MOTHERS, FATHERS, AND CHILDREN

The author with a group of children

MOTHERS, FATHERS, AND CHILDREN

Practical Advice to Parents

A. FURÚTAN

Translated from the Persian by
Katayoon and Robert Crerar

Child education is a matter of the utmost importance
'Abdu'l-Bahá

GEORGE RONALD
OXFORD

GEORGE RONALD, Publisher
46 High Street, Kidlington, Oxford, OX5 2 DN

ISBN 0 85398 094 2 (cloth)
ISBN 0 85398 095 0 (paper)

Printed in the United States of America

CONTENTS

vi

FOREWORD

THIS BOOK was written from my own experience as a child psychologist working with children and their mothers. It is a practical guide for mothers and fathers, not a scholarly presentation, although scholars and educators may perhaps find ideas in it which interest them. My intention was to help parents in their daily efforts to carry out the difficult task of training a child.

In writing the book I made use of ideas gathered from a study of the Bahá'í writings, the Bible, the Qur'án, philosophers such as Locke, Rousseau, Kant, Darwin, and Spencer, and the educationalists and child psychologists of our own day. I have not listed all the titles, but parents who are interested will be able to find a wealth of helpful information available from bookshops and libraries.

Originally written in Persian, the book has been edited for the Western reader. I should like to express my warm thanks to the translators, Katayoon and Robert Crerar, and to Mahnaz Aflatooni, who translated the extracts from Persian poetry. I should also like to thank the proof-readers, Ginnie Busey, Steve Eddy, Rustom Sabit, and Stephen Tomlin.

I

SIX EDUCATIONAL COUNSELS

According to the teachings of Bahá'u'lláh, the family being a human unit must be educated according to the rules of sanctity. All the virtues must be taught the family.[1]

THE GREAT PHILOSOPHER Herbert Spencer presented the family as the first unit of an organic society – a concept important to each of us as individuals. For just as discipline and laws are necessary for the establishment of justice and the advancement of civilization within a country, so should there be definite procedures and organization within a family, however small that family may be, so that its affairs may be managed smoothly, and equity and fairness be established in the home. In this way, the children will come to understand the true significance of discipline, order, responsibility, justice, and the protection of the rights of humanity. Without these, the foundation of children's education cannot be based on the teachings of the Divine Manifestations, the real Educators of the world of humanity.

This fundamental objective has been in the past a strong influence on the education of children, and will continue to be so in the future, sowing the seeds of humanity and civilization in their hearts. In recent years, many detailed studies of the family as a social unit have been conducted. The carefully considered opinions of experts, resulting from these studies, are of interest to parents, and some of them will be presented here.

The Necessity of Agreement between Parents

Ye were created to show love to one another and not perversity and rancour.[2]

In every family, the legislators, executives and judges are the fathers and mothers. Within the borders of the small and limited 'country' of the family, these three administrative powers are concentrated in the hands of the parents, who constantly enact rules and regulations for the children, having them carry out some actions, while preventing them from others; if differences arise amongst the children, the mother and father pass judgement.

1. The parents should determine, therefore, to reach mutual understanding on all aspects, whether trivial or important, of child raising. They should sincerely and systematically consult each other upon those matters which pertain to the training of their children and the fostering of their physical and spiritual well-being. After making thorough inquiries, and thinking carefully about the answers, the parents should set down rules and regulations within the family which are in complete accord with the spirit of proper training. If they are incapable of achieving this objective themselves, they should seek out the assistance of more competent and knowledgeable authorities, and, in full agreement, carry out the resulting decisions. The mother and father should never in any way whatso-

ever disagree about the treatment of their children and the management of the home, so that the children from early childhood consider themselves as being governed by one set plan of action, and see no differences of thought and opinion arising between the parents.

But if the mother and father are constantly disunited in their views on the upbringing of their children, if they dispute and argue and express opposing opinions in the presence of their offspring, then the children will be raised from the earliest years in an atmosphere of discord and incompatibility. The spirit of unity will disappear from the family, and the doors of felicity will be closed to their home. The children, naturally, will fall into two groups – one on the side of the father, and the other on the side of the mother. The proper education of children in such circumstances will be well-nigh impossible.

2. If thoughts and opinions concerning the training of children are not in harmony; if the father and mother incessantly argue, interfere in each other's affairs and responibilities, and are always finding fault; if the father issues orders contrary to those of the mother, and the mother goes against the guiding principles laid down by the father; – if this state of affairs exists within a family, then the children, bewildered, perplexed, and not knowing which course to pursue, will not put into practice the instructions of either parent, and will grow up to be obstinate, unscrupulous, and careless.

To clarify the matter, here is an example. A father sees nothing wrong with his thirteen-year-old daughter going to her friend's house, but the mother does not regard this as a proper thing to do, believing instead that a girl should not go out by herself. The parents have not discussed the question together, and do not share the same opinions on the subject.

The daughter asks her father's permission to go to her school friend's house. He answers, 'Yes, of course. Go ahead, dear.' The father, at this point, leaves the house. But when the girl wants to go, the mother prevents her from leaving, and becomes upset because of the 'improper' permission given by the father. She addresses her daughter: 'You won't dare set foot out of this house.' The girl answers that the father has granted her permission to leave. The mother angrily replies, 'Your father has made a mistake.'

The upshot of this scene has the daughter giving in to her mother, and giving up the idea of going to her friend's house. But later in the evening, when the father arrives home, the girl unlooses a torrent of complaints, thereby preparing the ground for an argument between the parents. Because his words have been 'thrown to the wind', the father becomes angry and resorts to arguing with his wife, who in order to protect her point of view, as well as her self-esteem, does not remain silent, but gives vent to everything she has on her mind. The situation winds up in the grip of a quarrel.

It is clear that the character of the children in such homes will ultimately deteriorate, because if, in the presence of the children, the father belittles and openly despises the mother, and lessens her worth in their sight:

1. The children become insolent and rude as they grow up, dominate their mother, and disobey her. They abase themselves in the sight of God, and disgrace themselves in the eyes of their fellow men.

2. The mother, in taking vengeance, resorts to back-biting about her husband and accuses him of being unreasonable, thereby instilling in the children strong feelings of hostility towards their father. She then belittles his station and reduces still further the respect which the children have for him; worst of all, she becomes deceitful, and creates fear in the children towards the father by depicting him as a tyrant.

For instance, the mother takes her child shopping and buys him a pair of shoes with money belonging to the father. She instructs the child that the matter should, at all costs, not be disclosed to the father, for if he finds out that the mother has bought new shoes, she explains, he will become so angry that he will 'shoot us both'. With occurrences such as this, it is clear what attitude the children will develop towards their father.

If the parents are always opposing each other, this will have a pernicious effect on the innocent children, depriving them of the sweetest and choicest fruit of life – the love of the mother and father. Being united in thoughts and views is therefore one of the top priorities of family life, and without it tranquillity and peace of mind are not possible.

Many parents ask their children unwise questions, and they want a specific answer. For instance, in front of the mother, the father asks his small child whom he loves best. Of course, he expects the child to prefer him to his mother. The child hesitates as he tries to find an answer. For several moments he remains silent, thinking that if he says he loves his father more, his mother will be hurt, and if he gives his mother the preference, his father will be offended. After a period of reflection, he gazes into the expectant eyes of the parents, and then quite wisely and confidently reports that he loves them both equally. Sadly, this clever answer fails to satisfy many inexperienced parents, and they insist that he choose one of them over the other. It is at this point that hypocrisy manifests itself in the child, and out of compulsion (and perhaps contrary to his opinion) he gives the preference to the one who provides him with greater material benefits. Although he may harbour more love for the mother, he nevertheless tells his father, 'Of course I love you more,' because of his material dependence on him, or from fear of his anger. Later, in the absence of the father, the mother scolds him and calls him ungrateful and disloyal. With perfect honesty the child says, 'Mother, of course I love you more than Father, but I had to say it the other way around so that Father would buy me new shoes. If I didn't say it that way, he wouldn't buy me the shoes.' Obviously, such treatment of children in a family is highly dangerous, and is bound to have undesirable consequences from the moral and educational point of view.

If love and affection govern the family, the father and mother are as united as one soul, and enjoy genuine intimacy: whatever words they may utter, whatever orders they may issue, and whatever instructions they may give, have previously been consulted upon and agreed between them, and demonstrate complete unity and sincere oneness. But in every family where estrangement reigns, the outcome will be darkness upon darkness: discord runs rampant among the children, and reverence for the parents is non-existent; sadness, sorrow, gloominess, and frustration manifest themselves at every turn; the thoughts and views of the mother and father are not in agreement, and each treats the other as a stranger – she hides her thoughts, words and actions from him, while he conceals his intentions and activities from her. She disparages him, while he regards her as less than nothing, belittling and despising her in the presence of the children; both of them spend their time thinking of their own personal advantage, on providing for the future and making ends meet.

It is evident, therefore, that the mother and father should be in agreement on all aspects of training, avoiding all manner of discord and contention, so that the affairs of the family may be managed in a well-disciplined and orderly fashion, based on sound principles.

The spirit of love and affection should radiate from the children, the light of oneness should burn brightly in their hearts, and the family environment should become like a rose-garden through this bounty; the children should look up to their parents with reverence, and not sense any disunity between them, so that as grown-ups they may become sincere servants to the world of humanity.

The Childhood Years and the Force of Habit

It is extremely difficult to teach the individual and refine his character once puberty is passed. By then, as experience hath shown, even if every effort be exerted to modify

*some tendency of his, it all availeth nothing. He may,
perhaps, improve somewhat today; but let a few days
pass and he forgetteth, and turneth backward to his
habitual condition and accustomed ways. Therefore it is
in early childhood that a firm foundation must be laid.
While the branch is green and tender it can easily be
made straight.*[3]

The period of human childhood is very long. Some
child psychologists consider children to be immature
until they reach the age of twelve, while others say
fourteen. They regard these years as the childhood
years. To quote the poet Ḥakím Niẓámí:

One day but seven years old you were,
like a flower trusted to the meadow you were,
but now that you are four and ten,
a cypress stretched towards heaven,
be not heedless, it is not the time for play,
it is the day to learn arts,
it is the day to exalt oneself.

Whereas a fish from the very first days of its life is
independent and in no need of help, such is not the case
with human offspring, who are helpless, powerless,
and dependent upon others for a long period of time.
There is great wisdom in the long duration of childhood, and every educator should be aware of it. If
parents do not give this subject the attention it deserves, they may forgo an extremely precious opportunity, and out of some lack of knowledge, unwittingly
make their little sweethearts bitter and dismal throughout their lives. Such parents are like those people who
neglect the principle of thrift, waste their resources and

capital, and in the end, distressed and powerless, are in need of hand-outs from others.

It is quite evident that the reason for the long period of childhood is to permit, under the guidance of educators, the strengthening of the physical and intellectual faculties, enabling the child to acquire essential learning and to gain those praiseworthy characteristics which are necessary for facing life (which is something very hard, and often bitter and unpleasant). Children gradually become prepared for the later stages of life, so that they can boldly meet the challenges of the world, and harmonize their natural instincts with the needs of society, which is awaiting them. In addition, they must have sufficient resources for the maturation of physical faculties (at twenty-five years) and spiritual faculties (at thirty-five years).

Experience has proved that a child learns easily from the educator before the age of maturity, but after that age, training and education become exceedingly difficult. That is, as we emerge from childhood and approach maturity, training becomes proportionally more complex. Teachers and parents should, therefore, make the most of the childhood years. They cannot waste this invaluable opportunity, aware as they are that every hour – nay, every minute – of these years has a specific purpose, and for every moment of childhood neglected, there will be deprivation in the future.

When a sailor decides to cross a dangerous stretch of water, he wastes no time in equipping his ship properly. In order to reach his destination safely, and that his ship may withstand gigantic waves without breaking apart in fierce storms, he must, of course, apply the necessary caution. By the same token, when parents steer the ship of the being of their precious children into the surging sea of social life, they should first make ready the requirements for reaching the shore of salvation, and provide those things which are necessary for the long and adventurous crossing.

Some parents do not give the period of childhood the attention it deserves, believing instead that children should be left to spend their time according to their own inclinations and demands, unopposed by anybody, in the hope that when they grow up, perception and understanding will automatically appear, and of their own account they will realize what they must do and how they should behave in society. Such parents are not unlike those gardeners who neglect to train a new shrub or trim its branches, hoping that the tree will correct itself as it grows and become stronger. The famous poet Sa'dí said,

> Happiness will flee whosoever
> is not trained in childhood.
> Reflect: The green branch can be guided,
> but the dry twig is straightened only by fire.

In order to derive the greatest benefit from childhood, it is not enough that children just go to school. At home and in society, too, they must be under complete care and spend their time in an orderly manner so that not even a minute of their precious time is wasted. Some child psychologists believe that even recreation and playtime should be planned according to scientific means. Inasmuch as the child is intuitively interested in playing, the educator should make full use of this natural interest. In this way, the child's spiritual and physical faculties are strengthened even through games, his time is not wasted, and his life is not fruitless. His brilliant light remains protected for its purpose of illuminating the dark night of life.

An important factor which should never be let out of the sight of parents and educators is the way in which habit plays a governing role in the lives of human beings. If we observe carefully, we will see that the expression 'It's become second nature' is in fact very accurate, because whatever a person gets used to, this somehow becomes his friendly companion until the end of his life, and it is troublesome and difficult to give it up.

It is not uncommon, for instance, for a person who has had a pocket watch for years to put his hand in his pocket involuntarily to search for the watch when he wants to know the time, in spite of having had it replaced by a wrist watch. Since he is perfectly aware of the change, why does this action occur? Simply because he has become so accustomed to having a pocket watch.

As another example, you are busy writing a letter, and the ink bottle is placed on your right. After writing a few lines, you transfer the ink container from the right to the left side of the table, and you continue writing. But when the pen runs dry, your hand automatically moves to the right, and when the nib clacks against the table top, you notice your error; still, you may make the same mistake several times, because of having reached to the right for several minutes before making the change.

If the force of habit is felt to such a degree that we get used to something after only a few minutes, then the period of childhood, which lasts for so many years, is unquestionably the most suitable time for the acquisition of good manners and pleasant habits. It was the opinion of the renowned philosopher John Locke that the inner tablet of a child is so simple and pure that a teacher, using education as his tool, can engrave on it anything he likes, irrespective of inherited characteristics. The remark has also been made that 'Knowledge received in childhood is like an engraving made on stone.'

There is no doubt that children are truly blessed if, through the care and attention of those entrusted with their upbringing, they learn praiseworthy conduct and shun blameworthy behaviour, and their childhood is spent in pursuing knowledge and human perfections, so that, when older, they may become fruitful trees – useful and progressive elements of society.

Parents' Words and Deeds are Children's Examples

Take heed, O people, lest ye be of them that give good counsel to others but forget to follow it themselves.[4]

It is only natural that, as parents, you should take a deep interest in the training and education of your children. You cherish the hope that they will grow up free from defilement, good-tempered, well-behaved, and deserving to take their place in society as civilized and progressive-minded human beings.

It is certain, for instance. that you prefer your children not to tell lies, not to backbite, and not to wrongly accuse others of misdeeds. You hope they will be honest and trustworthy, and will not sully their tongues with offensive and unpleasant talk. You expect them to show respect towards their parents, and, in short, to observe fully those moral principles which are conducive to the advancement of the human race, and to its distinction and happiness. If such be the case, then it is important to understand a delicate matter: this wish can only be realized when it is translated from thoughts into actions. In other words, you yourself must possess the very characteristics and perfections that you want your children to acquire, for in the view of the world's renowned scholars, the sayings and actions of parents exert a tremendous influence on their children. Experts are all united in the opinion that it is the parents who establish the morals and manners of their children, with the characteristics and virtues of the mother exerting a greater influence. Whatever the parents may do and whatever they may say (be it good or ill), will become a pattern for the child's conduct.

Many child psychologists believe that most of children's actions come about through imitation. This condition in children is so intense that we can compare the innermost self of a child to a mirror in which are reflected the actions and words of the father, mother, and others who come in contact with him.

From this, it can be readily understood that every action which the parents may carry out, and every word they may utter, will register a definite effect on the course of the child's training and education. For instance, if parents sincerely want their loved one to be truthful, not to backbite, not to neglect his prayers or other religious observances, not to defile his tongue with hideous expressions – if this represents the parents' earnest wish, then they themselves, in the home environment and in the presence of the child, must refrain from lying and malicious gossip, must recite prayers and obey daily the exhortations ordained by God, so that the child may follow their example, and be raised in an environment of spirituality, piety, and devotion.

For instance, however often you tell your child that lying is bad, that the liar degrades himself before others, and, as a famous Persian poet has said,

A lie makes a man undignified,
A lie brings him disgrace;

as soon as you utter a lie in front of a child, and as soon as he grasps the falsity of your words, all those counsels and advice will be forgotten, and like a morning mist that is dispelled by the first rays of sunlight, their effect will be immediately wiped from the child's inner being. And if your child becomes a partner in carrying out your lies, naturally your verbal counsels (which in any case rank as a weak educational tool) will be effaced much more quickly.

Picture, for example, a father dutifully advising his child never to tell lies. At this point, someone drops in to see the father, but he sends the child to tell the caller that he is not at home. Consider: Will those counsels have the slightest moral effect on that child? Will they sow the seeds of trustworthiness in his heart, soul, and conscience?

Whatever parents say to their children, and whatever they guide them to do, they themselves should mirror forth those same moral guide-lines in their daily lives. Otherwise, their verbal counsels, unaccompanied by action, will produce no result whatever except to waste time.

Many parents mistakenly think that their young children 'will never understand these things'. On the contrary, in addition to the sense of imitation, the sense of curiosity is so strong in children that invariably they wish to know about everything: they cling to every word, and are thorough in every matter, according to their capacity and understanding. Nothing remains hidden from the microscopic sight of such a sensitive, active, thorough, and curious creature, (of course, according to his talent and level of comprehension) who is far from lacking in ability and intelligence. The point is that he looks at those around him through his own eyes, and interprets and judges what he sees and hears according to his own understanding and perception.

Consider for a moment how water, from the instant it is placed on the fire, begins gathering heat, and continues warming up until it reaches boiling point; that is, for a certain period of time it warms up, but finally it boils. The same analogy applies to children, as from childhood whatever they see or hear is collected and stored until, at the appointed time, it is made manifest.

Fathers and mothers should be consciously aware that their children are carefully watching their every act and deed, and comprehending everything according to their own level of understanding and intelligence, even though they do not often explicitly express their feelings, thoughts, and opinions.

It often happens that the parents – believing their child to be sound asleep, and seeing themselves unhampered – talk about things that they would not discuss in the presence of the child. The parents are certain that they are acting wisely, and that statements which could have a negative effect on the child are not being uttered in his presence. But in the morning, when the child relates that same conversation to her, the mother discovers that he was pretending to sleep, overheard every word and recorded it all in his pure heart. He went to sleep pondering those very words, having absorbed the entire incident in his soul.

The parents should always be alert and maintain constant vigilance over their words and actions; nor may this precaution be relaxed when the children are supposed to be asleep. They should not consider children to be bereft of understanding, for whatever action the parents may undertake, and whatever words they may utter, the children will take them as their example. If these words and actions are reasonable and correct, the results will be beneficial; if they are unreasonable and incorrect, the effects are bound to be detrimental.

Self-control

The individual must be educated to such a high degree that he . . . would think it easier to be slashed with a sword or pierced with a spear than to utter calumny or be carried away by wrath.[5]

People who are quick to anger and who are easily provoked usually do not exercise restraint over what they think and say, and cannot, because of their nervous state, make use of this counsel of Sa'dí:

Reflect before speaking your thoughts,
foundations precede building the walls,
whosoever ponders not his words,
his reply is often unsuitably expressed.

As a result, strong words are often uttered during a spell of rage or anger – words which would not be said under normal conditions. When the state of inner turmoil subsides, and the people afflicted are once again calm and collected, they deeply regret what they have done, but, of course, 'it's always too late to change the past.'

Such situations are regrettable from the viewpoint of training and education, as they have lamentable effects on children. How often has it happened that a few improper words falling from the lips of a father or mother have altered the course of a child's life and led him into utter loss.

Picture a situation in which hard feelings have erupted between a father and mother, and their love and affection for each other have been replaced by estrangement. The wife has, for various reasons, been offended by her husband, and as a result, anger builds up in her heart. Eventually her pent-up feelings explode, and she verbally assails her husband and slanders his behaviour. By this time, the children have gathered around, and are listening to everything. And the mother, out of anger, gives vent to thoughts which she does not even regard as being true, and which she would never say in normal circumstances.

She may for example, say: 'Look at the wretch I have for a husband – so well-off and healthy, and I am made to feel so miserable and unhappy all the time. If there were really a God who punished people for their crimes, then my husband wouldn't be as you see him today, and I wouldn't be in such a miserable state with no one to help me, or even to ask me how I am.'

If, in the midst of all this, a sympathetic friend tells her that the truth is otherwise, and that she is saying things she does not mean, because of her feelings of anger, the lady, in the same anguished manner, with tears running down her cheeks, vehemently replies: 'Who can believe in God and in an afterlife? These are only words! If there were a God he would punish my husband and take him off my hands.'

The children, who are standing nearby, are both disturbed and saddened by this state of affairs. But they are strongly influenced by the mother's words, and think to themselves that what she has said must, in fact, be true. It is evident that the seeds of irreligious-ness and carelessness are, in this way, planted in the soil of the children's hearts, and these will grow and yield fruits too bitter to imagine or describe.

When the mother overcomes her angry feelings and calms her nerves, she attempts to make her children understand that the truth of the matter is contrary to what she said before. But this attempt will prove futile, for her words have already produced a reaction, and the lethal poison has begun to take effect.

Parents should at least try to control their anger in front of children so as not to say things that may prove harmful to them. It does no good to say, 'When we get angry, we have no control over what we do or say.' The presence of children should serve as a reminder to the mother and father that they are not at liberty to act as they please. Just as a person attempts to control his emotions in front of other people, so should he control his anger in the presence of children.

Keeping Promises Made to Children

Trustworthiness is the greatest portal leading unto the tranquillity and security of the people. In truth the stability of every affair hath depended and doth depend upon it.[6]

A quality whose foundation should be established in children at an early age is that of being faithful to promises and abiding by one's word. If individuals in a society are faithful to their covenants and respect all their agreements, the doors of trustworthiness will be opened wide to the members of that society; beneficial concerns will be established, and a myriad hardships and obstacles will be uprooted from their midst.

We are all familiar with unfulfilled promises and how they are a continual source of trouble, and with what unusual force they interrupt the normal flow of affairs in society, and to what extent everyday work falls into disorder and society becomes disrupted. Day and night, complaints can be heard about people who have failed to keep their promises. You order a pair of boots from a shoemaker who tells you the day and the hour that they will be ready. After returning then and on subsequent occasions, only to have the date repeatedly postponed until 'tomorrow', you eventually receive the finished product. Tailors, dressmakers, watchmakers, opticians, merchants – in short, all strata of society – are afflicted with this deadening social disease, the breaking of promises.

If one day we wish to be rid of this ailment, we must take steps now to administer the cure, and instil in our children (who will take our places in society) such a desire for keeping their word that they will unhesitatingly shun the deplorable habit of breaking promises. The most direct route to this goal consists in this: children should never see their parents evading or breaking promises. Regrettably, most fathers and mothers give this point little consideration and base the relationship which they have with their young children on unkept promises. Rarely do they keep their word with youngsters. With their own hands they lay the groundwork for this damaging habit in the inner-beings of their loved ones, raising them to be un-motivated to keep their promises and abide by their words.

Suppose a young child is following his mother around the house, watching her as she prepares to go out. He is crying, since he wants to accompany her. In order to quieten him the mother promises him that if he stays at home and behaves himself and does not cry, she will buy him some toys or perhaps some candies from a nearby confectioner's. When the mother is making these promises, she knows perfectly well that she will probably forget to keep them; her only pur-pose is to keep the child quiet for the moment. She considers this trick necessary to stop him crying. The 'simple' child has been taken in on previous occasions by his mother's misleading promises, but once again he believes her words and, with a tranquil mind, stays at home. He wipes away his tears and tries especially hard to be happy, lest his mother find any fault with him; he is completely loyal to his side of the agreement and becomes a quiet and well-behaved child, all the while counting the minutes until he gets his reward of toys and candies. Finally, the waiting period – which to him is akin to death – is over, and he hears his mother's footsteps coming up the walk. Breathlessly, he rushes to greet her. Looking first to see if she is carrying anything, he blurts, 'Mum, did you buy a toy? Did you bring some candies?' The drama concludes with the mother making a great but hypocritical display of surprise, as she sighs a deep sigh and clasps her hands together saying, 'Oh, no! I forgot! Listen to what happened. I ran into one of our neighbours and we started talking and the entire matter slipped my mind. I have made a mistake. But don't worry! The next time I go downtown I'll buy them for you for sure.'

Whoever is able to remember such episodes from his childhood is aware of the hurt and anger which result, and the burning indignation that lingers long afterwards.

The reactions to unkept promises vary: some children scream, while others weep quietly. Some accuse their mothers, saying, 'Don't tell lies. You remembered it, but you didn't want to spend the money.' And so it goes. But the end result is similar for all children: because of repeated bouts with broken promises, they draw the conclusion, 'There is nothing wrong with failing to keep a promise, since many fathers and mothers do not always do what they say they will. If it were so bad,' the children reason, 'then parents would never be parties to it.' (This may help the reader to understand the consequences of this approach.)

I once witnessed an exchange in which a grandfather, about to go to the market-place, was asked by his three-year-old grandchild in his childish language to bring him something back. The grandfather said, 'When I come back, I will bring you a treat.' When he returned, the bright-eyed child ran to greet him and, in the same childish language, asked hopefully, 'Did you bring the treat? Where is it?' Even though the grandfather saw himself in the wrong, he carelessly shrugged off the matter with a simple 'I forgot to buy it'. The poor child was so thunderstruck that just looking at him involuntarily aroused my pity.

Parents and others who deal with children should have no doubt that failure to keep promises has a detrimental effect on children's training. Every attempt should be made to avoid this unjust action. Either promises should not be made, or, if they have been made, they should definitely and without exception be carried through to fulfilment. Before promising anything to a child the parents should first judge whether or not it can be fulfilled. If they are able to keep their promises, well and good, but they should never use them as a tool to deceive the child, for in doing so, they commit two serious errors:

1. They have not carried out what they said they would.

2. They have sown in the heart of the child the seed of the blameworthy habit of not keeping one's promises; in time this seed will germinate and grow to maturity, and its thorns will be the cause of many problems.

The Effects of Deceit on Children

Truthfulness is the foundation of all the virtues of the world of humanity. Without truthfulness, progress and success in all the worlds of God are impossible for a soul. When this holy attribute is established in man, all the divine qualities will also become realized.[7]

'O, I am so weary of children.' 'These children have ruined the best years of my life.' 'My children don't even give me time to catch my breath.'

Such are the complaints that mothers tend to voice to anyone and everyone they come in contact with, thereby making one and all aware that they have completely run out of patience with their children.

In order to get away from the 'mischievousness' of the children and have a rest, mothers employ different tactics, most of which are contrary to divine will, and go against educational guide-lines; they cling to these methods because they see no alternatives, and because they are unfamiliar with correct methods. Deceit is one of the methods used: mothers trick their children so as to gain temporary respite from them.

Consider this example, in which a mother wants to go to the cinema, but does not want to take her young child along. As the mother is preparing to leave, the child asks where she is going. The answer is: 'I am not feeling well, and I must pay a visit to the doctor and get a prescription for some medicine to help me get better.' The child, judging from the mother's outward appearance – her countenance, bright eyes, and spry movements – has suspicions about the truth of her statements from the very first. But then, in his innermost thoughts, he concedes the possibility that this time, she may have told the truth. After she has left, however, and the little boy is by himself, within the confines of his childish mind he starts thinking about and analyzing his mother's statements: he perceives that her red cheeks, bright eyes, and state of joy are not at all like those of a sick person, and nobody so happy and cheerful goes to visit the doctor.

Impatiently, he awaits her return. He notices that she comes in very late, and the fact that she has no medicine with her confirms his suspicions.

Very carefully, but with doubt in his voice, the child asks, 'Mum, did you go to the doctor?'

In order to cover up her previous lie, the mother resorts to other false statements, and says that she was unable to visit the doctor, because on the way, she ran into such-and-such a person, who said this and that, and made her go to her house. But by this time, the mother has let the cat out of the bag, as the saying goes, and is disgraced in front of her young child. It even becomes clear to her that her lies have been discovered. Such situations are obviously harmful to children.

A child once excitedly described the following incident to me. One day, a mother took her son to the cinema, but told her daughter that she was taking him to the dentist to have a tooth treated. When they returned home, the girl was in bed, pretending to be asleep. The mother called her name several times. When she received no answer, she assumed that her daughter had fallen into a deep sleep; then she proceeded to tell her husband about the afternoon spent at the cinema with their son. In her 'sleep', the daughter learnt about everything that happened, and in the morning, told her mother: 'Mum, last night I dreamt that you took my brother to such-and-such a film, and then bought this, that and the other for him.'

Incidents of this nature unquestionably worsen the morals of children, and do so to an extent which cannot be assessed. This habit should be totally uprooted from families, because lying and its attendant effects are more devastating than all other evils. Lies are harmful whether they are told to grown-ups or children.

Parents should train their children in such a way that lying is never needed. When they wish to do something, or when they have to leave the house for some reason, they must tell the truth of the matter, and not make themselves captive to any inappropriate demands of the children. They should rear their children in such a way that deceit, imposture and craftiness will never be experienced within the family environment. 'They should endeavour', wrote Shoghi Effendi, 'to inculcate, gently and patiently, into their youthful minds such principles of moral conduct and initiate them into the principles and teachings of the Cause with such tactful and loving care as would enable them to become "true sons of God" and develop into loyal and intelligent citizens of His Kingdom. This is the high purpose which Bahá'u'lláh Himself has clearly defined as the chief goal of every education.'[8]

2

RESPECT FOR CHILDREN

Know ye not why We created you all from the same dust? That no one should exalt himself over the other. Ponder at all times in your hearts how ye were created.[1]

I admonish you to observe courtesy, for above all else, it is the prince of virtues. . . . Whoso is endued with courtesy hath indeed attained a sublime station.[2]

MOST OF US know from experience that the hearts of children are by nature very delicate. Their feelings are sensitive, and although we may not be aware of it, their views on those matters which affect themselves are perceptive. We can compare the delicacy of children's hearts to flower petals, and the sensitivity of their feelings to clear water, while the acuteness of their vision reminds us of a strong microscope: the first will wither and fade away at the first sign of rough handling, the second will be clouded and polluted by the least amount of agitation, while the third will make them keen-sighted and precise.

It is unfortunate that some parents, instead of treating their children with gentleness, civility, compassion, and affection, act harshly and in a fiery manner towards them. It can generally be stated that families in every stratum of society are afflicted to some degree with this calamitous attitude.

Many fathers and mothers have little consideration

for the dignity of young children – that is to say, they do not accord them full status as human beings. Their reasoning follows this pattern: children's bodies are small and their physical strength is undeveloped, so their feelings and expectations are of little account. This incorrect approach – the falsity of which both science and experience have long since proven – repeatedly leads parents to deal harshly with their children, treat them without respect, and often hurt their tender feelings. By this kind of behaviour, parents inflict severe harm on their loved ones, and damage their own dignity and station as well.

It is characteristic of children to be sensitive, easily offended, and tender-hearted. But at the same time, they are very egotistical and demanding, and the slightest sign of unkindness torments their delicate and sensitive hearts, and saddens their souls. When the father and mother do not respect their child, and show no consideration for him, the child immediately feels hurt. If he is repeatedly offended, his nerves become feeble and weak, causing him sadness and sorrow. He becomes accustomed to discourtesy and abuse so that, little by little, he ceases to be troubled by harsh words or offensive deeds, and, as the parents say, he becomes 'thick-skinned'. When a child becomes extremely sad, his grief will exhaust him physically, and make him indifferent to abuse and degradation. Here is an example to clarify this point:

In the face of a child's questions and demands, a mother responds harshly with expressions such as 'shut up,' 'drop dead,' 'go and get lost,' 'don't talk so much,' 'don't be nosey,' and so on. A child who is unaccustomed to hearing such expressions feels hurt, and in the intensity of his sorrow, he cries, for such talk does not befit his dignity. After a few days, however, the child gets used to hearing these words, and scolding and censure no longer have any effect. The mother is obliged to intensify her approach by using still more repugnant expressions and increasingly coarse statements. But after a while, the child gets used to these words too, necessitating a further escalation in the mother's harshness. As this curve spirals upwards, it will reach the stage of swearing at the child and vilifying him, which we will discuss later.

If the mother had shown respect towards her child from the first, and had totally avoided, in accordance with Scripture, the use of harsh or ugly words, then the child, at the slightest sign of disapproval from his parents, would have come to recognize his faults and curtail his unpleasant behaviour. Experienced parents who are aware of these points deal with their children with the utmost respect, and say things of this nature to them: 'My, but you are behaving yourself well.' 'If your behaviour continues like this, you will be a good example to others.' 'Thank you for keeping your promise.' 'You know how much your mother will feel annoyed if you do this again?'

Of course, children must be treated according to their ages, but to go into detail is not possible in this short presentation of the subject. The principal and indisputable educational point, however, is that children must be treated with the utmost courtesy, and every attempt should be made to avoid making them the object of harsh words. Under whatever conditions fathers and mothers may find themselves, they should never overstep the bounds of courtesy and dignity, nor conclude that children are dull and ignorant because they are young and lacking in ability. Quite the contrary: they have feelings and sentiments and a sense of honour, and believe in and adhere to whatever dignity the childhood world permits. In the same way that grown-ups loathe being insulted and degraded, so children despise discourtesy and insults which, if they are used frequently, will have irreversible consequences.

Avoid Harsh Treatment

The child must not be oppressed or censured because it is undeveloped; it must be patiently trained.[3]

1. A mother is nursing her infant. The baby, unconscious of almost everything, has nuzzled against its mother's bosom, and expects nothing but kindness and affection. It so happens that the feeble child has stomach cramps and is unable to drink the milk. As it cries and squirms, the mother of that angelic and tiny creature unlooses a flood of anger. She spanks and abuses the infant, and if the crying continues for a long time, leaves it to itself in a corner.

2. A child has reached the stage of learning to talk. In his childish way, he asks endless questions, and refuses to separate himself from his mother, following her everywhere like a shadow. Her patience begins to wear thin. By the time he has made the house untidy and turned everything upside-down, the mother's anger will lead her to punish the child for his 'nosiness'.

3. A number of grown-ups are sitting around talking, laughing, and telling stories. For the most part, they are having a good time. In their midst, a child is sitting and listening intently to their conversation. Because he is not able to understand the subjects being

discussed, he often interrupts in order to have something explained or repeated. Since the adults consider him a nuisance and do not allow him any rights whatever in their gatherings (or for that matter, in society), they belittle and abuse him so severely that he is driven away. The tender heart of the wronged child will be bruised and his sensitive soul darkened. Inevitably he heads for a corner and cries loudly; in future, he will shun such gatherings.

Children of families like these, instead of being full of joy and happiness, often spend their childhood years in a state of sadness and despair, regularly experiencing feelings of bitterness and gloom. Some young children are surrounded by happy faces and laughter, natural landscapes, springs, mountains, meadows, fields, and forests; they attend exhibitions and cultural institutions, and read interesting and educational books; they receive nothing but sweet smiles, affectionate glances, kind treatment and sweet words; and they are trained, reminded and corrected with the utmost skill and with the use of tested and proven methods. It is to be regretted that other children are exposed to nothing but harshness and violence from their parents and from others with whom they come in contact; they have no safe place to take a walk or a run, nor do they have access to special books and films suitable to their age. These children are like prisoners whose cells are cramped and dark, and whose gaolers are bad-tempered and grim-faced.

Such a state of affairs is harmful and dangerous both to the bodies and minds of children, and introduces into society weak, sick, nervous, bad-tempered, and pessimistic individuals who possess countless physical and spiritual defects, and who, little by little, will lead that society to ruin and utter loss.

Parents, educators and others who deal with children must, therefore, realize that:

1. Young children do have feelings and emotions and possess the capacity for thought and intellectual activity, the only difference being that these faculties are in their initial stages of growth, and can be likened to fresh plants in need of training by a skilful gardener so as to grow and develop fully – and not of being continually irritated, or of having their roots sundered with an axe, or their trunks scarred with knives, or their branches and leaves plucked out by force and scattered to the four winds.

2. To break a child's heart to no avail, to disregard and pay no attention to him, to offend him without reason – these are serious errors and constitute grave sins. Parents should never be willing to see tears of sadness welling from a child's eyes and running down his cheeks.

3. If children are offended by the parents and consider themselves the object of their cruelty, little by little the love and affection which they feel towards the father and mother will be transformed into hatred and revenge; the foundation of that family will be weakened, and its structure of unity will collapse. No shock is more severe to the family structure than being heedless of children's feelings.

4. If parents want to educate children and rectify their shortcomings, they must make use of scientific principles and techniques, and must not for a moment

succumb to the belief that forcible and violent means are the only ways open to them.

As far as possible, children's years of training should be wreathed in happy smiles, pleasant and compassionate words, love and affection. Why should they be made to cry, or be made sad and gloomy? Are not sweet smiles, ringing laughter, and happy and joyful faces preferable to crying eyes, sighs, groans, and bitter wailing? Let us make a covenant to be no cause of grief to our innocent children, and to bring them up as happy and joyful beings.

Verbal Abuse, Threats, and Physical Punishment

It is not, however, permissible to strike a child, or vilify him, for the child's character will be totally perverted if he be subjected to blows or verbal abuse.[4]

Love and kindness have far greater influence than punishment upon the improvement of human character.[5]

We are all fully aware of the prevalence of threats and verbal abuse within many family environments. When mothers run out of patience with their children's disobedience and naughtiness, they usually resort to the weapons of the weak – hollow threats, abuse and curses. This practice has become so entrenched among educators and parents alike, regardless of their social status or level of education, that without any forethought whatsoever they give vent to expressions such as, 'I wish you had never been born!' 'If you say that once more I'll cut your tongue off!' 'We'll throw you to the wolves!' 'Do that again and I'll beat you to within an inch of your life!' 'May God punish you for that!' 'I'll break every bone in your body!' 'I'll wallop the daylights out of you!' 'May you never live to see another day!'

Such an approach has innumerable harmful effects on children, some of which will be pointed out here.

A. *The harmful effects of verbal abuse.*

One of the counsels of scholars is that an educator must never vilify children, because this, along with the use of unkind and coarse expressions, destroys a child's sense of shame, and gradually effaces his self-respect, leading him to act insolently towards his educators (whether parents or teachers). As time goes on, the child is hardly affected by swearing and verbal abuse. Gradually he starts using the same foul words with his peers, and finally his discourtesy intensifies to such a degree that he will not shrink from using abusive language to his teachers, and even to his parents.

It has often happened that a child will quietly bear, for a certain period of time, the verbal abuse and slander of his parents, but when his patience has borne all that it can bear, and he is stripped of the veil of his sense of shame, then brute anger overcomes him, and the dross of impoliteness obscures the radiance of his heart. He will then treat his parents as he himself was treated, and those same indecent phrases and vulgar words will revert to the mother and father.

It has often been observed that a child may derive satisfaction from seeing his parents suffer, thus calming his sense of retaliation and extinguishing the fire of his anger. More important than anything is that at first, ugly or indecent phrases are mere words to the child, but later on, as a result of frequent usage, he will discover their meanings. Finally, he will fall so deeply into the slough of corruption that all doors leading to his rescue are firmly barred. For this reason, teachers of morality have discouraged the use of indecent language.

When parents wish to deter their children from offensive deeds, under no circumstances should they resort to swearing and verbal abuse. They must be aware that the practice of giving vent to obscenities has no scientific support as a means of rectifying a child's behaviour. Not only will it corrupt the child's morals, but in his heart, strong feelings of vengeance towards the abusive party will be created. The day will come when these pent-up feelings will erupt and drive the child to take revenge.

Swearing is, in fact, a kind of malevolence, an invoking of divine torment and punishment. If young children, through their defective thinking, consider parents to be their ill-wishers and see them as unkind or hateful, day by day their love and affection, faithfulness and sincerity towards their parents will diminish; they will not only be disobedient, but the seeds of hatred and animosity will be sown in their hearts. And if fathers and mothers persist in meting out harsh treatment and offending their children with indecent expressions, the fabric of friendship and intimacy which should always exist between parent and child will be torn apart, and arrogance and pertness will increasingly manifest themselves in the children.

Besides all this, the reviling of children, the uttering of curses and the invoking of punishment are far from the love and kindness which are the child's spiritual birthright. Even though mothers may truly claim that such phrases are not to be taken literally and are only said out of habit, nevertheless the influence of words and deeds can never be denied, and every word exerts a definite effect. A prudent person first attempts to discuss what the outcome of his actions will be, that is, 'to see the end in the beginning'. Since the only result of verbal abuse is harm to the minds and bodies of the children, it is better for parents to do away with this blameworthy practice and deal with their children in such a manner as to attract them and make them enamoured with their parents, who will then have no need to resort to violence and harshness.

Parents, and especially mothers, can win the hearts of their children through the use of gentle words, and kind and affectionate language. During times of difficulty, hardship, psychological stress, and inner suffering, they will come to be regarded by their children as friends and companions, and as a place of refuge; the children will confide in and not flee from them. But if a child detests his mother and father, and if, in his eyes, they are cruel, tyrannical, and overbearing, then a fearful breach is created between the parents and their offspring. This situation could deteriorate to the degree that the child might turn his back on hearth and home. Putting aside kindness and family love, he might even consider the family itself as an enemy, and seek out the companionship of others (who may not be his well-wishers) in order to unburden his heart.

Of course, we all know that in any home where the parents are strict without any logical reason, where they treat their children unkindly and do not agree to their legitimate desires, the children will gradually become disillusioned. Because of intense anguish and frustration, they will avoid home (if they have no other choice) and become disobedient and rebellious towards their parents.

Our children are like young plants in the garden of the assemblage of mankind. They are in dire need of our affection and kind-heartedness, our friendship and sympathy. Educators, therefore, should not swear or use verbal abuse, nor should they break the children's sensitive and delicate hearts; rather, they should treat them with the utmost kindness and patience, and should use logical and scientific methods (approved by educationalists) to rectify their conduct. The training of children is not an easy undertaking, nor is it to be done according to each and every person's feelings and inclinations.

B. The harmful effects of threats
Hollow and fruitless threats are no less harmful than verbal abuse. When a mother threatens a child with punishment but does not put it into practice, the children soon discover that her words and threats are not going to be carried out, and that her only purpose is to frighten them. In such cases, the admonitions of the parents will fall on deaf ears.

In addition, exaggerated threats can never be put into practice, and are usually derided and mocked by the children, thereby reducing the station of the educator in their sight. For instance, when a mother is furious, she says such things as: 'I'd like to put your head on the chopping block,' or 'I'll knock you into the middle of next week,' or 'We'll put you through the meat-grinder,' and the child to whom these words are addressed has no alternative but to laugh, for the idea of any of these things happening seems funny to him.

A moral principle that has been emphasized and re-emphasized by all the Divine Manifestations, by the sages and the learned of every nation and every cultural background, is that one should not say something which he cannot put into action. When a person says that he will carry out a certain task and afterwards does not do it, he becomes known amongst his associates as someone who does not keep his word.

One of the human virtues and a noble characteristic is that of being faithful to one's words and promises. When children from their earliest years see how their mothers and fathers threaten them with things whose realization is impossible, they will cease paying attention to other promises made by their parents as well, and will consider their talk to be idle and non-sensical. Little by little, they themselves will acquire these twin habits of promise-breaking and idle talk.

If the object of threats and abuse is to train children and divert them from wrong-doing, then parents will never succeed so long as they employ this method; and if the purpose is to frighten the children, then once again, the task cannot be accomplished by this method. Fathers and mothers should, therefore, dispense with this useless and detrimental habit altogether.

Children should be trained in the home in such a way that the slightest lack of attention from the mother or father is in itself the greatest punishment. This goal can only be achieved through kindness and the use of soft speech. The greater the intimacy between parent and child, and the less the children are offended by the use of unbecoming language, the more fully the main goal – the training and education of the morals of children – can be realized.

And if on occasion the parents are obliged to warn and caution their children with reasonable punishment (provided that the punishment has been carefully evaluated beforehand) then they should definitely keep their word and put into action whatever they have said. To neglect to do this will render future warnings meaningless to the children. If, for instance, the parents tell a child that he will not be permitted to go out with them because he has not done a certain task and was negligent in carrying out such-and-such an instruction, then they must translate their words into action and refuse to take him even if he resorts to crying and screaming. If the persistence of the child wins out and causes the parents to feel pity for him and take him out with them, thereby nullifying their own warning, then this preventive measure will have no influence on the child on future occasions.

It is essential that the parents pay due attention to these points, for even though these matters may seem unimportant at first glance, fathers and mothers should consider them carefully because of the influence which they will have on later stages of their children's lives.

C. *The harmful effects of physical punishment*
Subjecting a child to blows is no less harmful than swearing and verbal abuse. Most educationalists believe that striking children totally perverts and destroys their characters. Ever since the sixteenth century (that is, following the death of Martin Luther, who made valuable contributions to this subject) scholars

such as John Locke, Sir Thomas More, Komenský, and hundreds of other knowledgeable people in this field have regarded child-beating as an abomination, and have admonished instructors and parents to avoid this contemptible action. Since the beginning of the twentieth century, even the conception of such an idea in the minds of most educators is not permissible.

Many people who train animals believe that even they should not be beaten, but dealt with according to scientifically-proven methods of training. The same applies to children. Those who consider beating, physical punishment, and even spanking to be occasionally necessary are not adequately informed about scientifically-sound methods. When these people find themselves unable to cope with their children, they cling to this weapon – an approach the falsity of which is upheld by the science of child psychology. This science, while counselling educators not to use force and coercion, urges them to increase their awareness of the psychological make-up of the intricate and marvellous being that is the child, and to acquire the key to the locked doors of the child's soul, so as to open the gates to these mysteries easily, and not have to break them apart.

The harmful effects of physical punishment are innumerable, and brevity would not be well served by relating them all here. To summarize, however, striking a child can make him obstinate and rude, and create a lingering vengeance in his heart; little by little, it subdues his self-respect, and renders counsels and advice ineffective, leading the educator to devise even more severe means of punishment. The mistreated child, constantly punished and tormented by the ignorant educator, becomes so deprived of developing kind-heartedness and tender and delicate feelings that gradually he will change into a revengeful and brutal individual with the heart of a stone. It is obvious that if the number of such people increases in a society, this will become a major cause of anxiety among those who are devoted to the progress of that society. It was Rousseau's opinion that a child has by nature been created very good, and that the hand of the educator should not alter the natural disposition and temperament or change his intrinsic characteristics, otherwise he will impel the child towards perversity and immorality.

The Effects of Frightening Children

. . . under no circumstances whatsoever should we assume any attitude except that of gentleness and humility.[6]

The custom of frightening children in order to quieten them is another habit that has spread to every stratum of society, and through excessive use has become second nature to a great number of people.

Picture this all-too-common scene, in which a young child is restless and fidgety, and is screaming to high heaven because of stomach trouble, a headache, teething problems and the like. The mother tries various means to calm him. When these produce no result, she recalls what her own nanny or mother used to do in similar circumstances, and resorts to scaring the wits out of him: she either acts like a wild beast, summoning up all sorts of blood-curdling howls, or she tells the child, 'The wolf is coming.' In doing this, the mother cherishes the hope that perhaps her 'inconsiderate' child will pity her and stop screaming. If this approach fails, the mother lets loose such a loud and callous roar that the child's face instantly grows pale, his sensitive heart palpitates, his body quivers, and he comes close to fainting.

A method employed by other mothers and nannies is to mask themselves, add appropriate sound effects, and crawl on hands and knees towards the trembling children; the fear and terror which this generates almost drives these smallest of angels insane. Concocting frightening stories with leading rôles for elves, hobgoblins, evil spirits, ghosts, and devils is yet another weapon used to instil fear in children.

The principal cause of this harmful habit is insufficient knowledge about the minds and bodies of young children. The habit itself is deeply rooted among people whose preparation for child-rearing is inadequate.

It is essential that girls be taught the fundamentals of the physiology and psychology of children so that when they become mothers they will be able to make full use of the vast amount of literature about child-raising that is at the disposal of parents. 'Shall they who have knowledge and they who have it not, be treated alike?' asks the Qur'án.

Mothers who have even a little knowledge about the minds and bodies of children can be compared to people who walk with clear vision in the light of the sun, easily distinguishing the straight path from trails strewn with brambles and pitfalls; mothers who remain unaware of the teachings of the science of child-raising are like those who must grope their way along with bleary eyes, all the while exposed to innumerable difficulties and dangers.

Instead of trying to frighten children who are restless and fidgety, parents ought to ascertain the causes of their behaviour. They should be quite sure that a child does not cry, scream or whine without reason. If a child's state of unrest is prolonged and the mother is unable to find the cause, then she ought to arrange for a doctor to see him. The practice of creating feelings of terror in children does immeasurable damage; carried to excess, it will have irreversible effects. Such tactics not only terrify children, but weaken their nerves, cause their imaginations to run wild, and decrease their courage: they become terrified of darkness, and are hesitant to step out of the house without someone accompanying them; thunder, lightning, the wind, rainfall – anything to which they are unaccustomed fills them with fear. Not even during sleep do their nervous systems let them relax; eerie dreams jolt them awake, and screaming and crying, they complain to their parents about the frightful nightmares. Many a night these children have no peace and beg their mothers not to leave them by themselves, but to hold their hands so they can sleep.

It is clear that children who are frightened to excess in childhood will not in adolescence and adulthood have adequate courage to meet the many decisions and trials which they are bound to face in life. A summary of this discussion must needs underline the detrimental and pernicious effects which this practice has on children's minds and bodies, and recommend that such an approach be totally done away with in all families.

Moderation in Joking

In all matters moderation is desirable. If a thing is carried to excess, it will prove a source of evil.[7]

'Joking is to speaking as salt is to eating,' goes a famous Arabic saying from the past. And just as food to which too much salt has been added becomes inedible, so it is with joking, which becomes unpalatable when it goes too far. It often happens that something said in jest produces discord, dissension and displeasure, and firmly establishes a foundation of hostility between members of a group.

Adults joke not only with one another – and occasionally the comments become heavy or are accompanied by coarse or harsh words – but often with children as well. When greeting a child, they speak facetiously; they do not refrain even in front of the child's father, mother, peers and friends, addressing him in words which do not reflect the courtesy of polite and dignified people. This approach has many detrimental effects on the development of children, some of which are listed here:

1. When joking is carried too far, both the person doing the joking and the one who is listening will overstep the bounds of courtesy and dignity. The child will gradually become rude, insolent, and cheeky towards grown-ups; the value and station of the person joking will be eroded in his sight, and he will not feel obliged to show any respect towards his superiors.

2. This action will also lead the innocent child into impropriety; he will become so used to joking that it will become one of his habits, and injury may result from his offensive words.

3. Experience has proven that joking is one of those habits which lead to excess; in this way it resembles gambling. That is to say, when a person says something jokingly which is enjoyed by those present, he will be encouraged to continue. Then he may say something stronger so as to be more popular. If he fails, he will try even harder in order to make up for his failure, and in the hope of success, he will advance still further into the field of combat. This process will, of course, have a detrimental effect.

4. Developing the habit of joking and jesting attracts children and adolescents towards buffoonery and introduces them to society as light-minded, undignified and discourteous individuals.

5. When children are shown no respect by other people, and let their delicate and sensitive hearts be injured by sarcastic words (which they do not realize are meant to be a joke), their souls will become saddened and vexed; they will get accustomed to insults and abuse, and little by little, they will lose their individuality. This loss in itself will have innumerable pernicious effects on their future development.

Improper jesting, or, in other words, the teasing of childen, should therefore be done away with altogether. When adults meet children and want to talk with them, instead of teasing them or treating them as inferiors, they should converse with them with the utmost love, affection, respect, politeness, and dignity, and in simple language, in accordance with their capacities and levels of comprehension, increase their limited knowledge as much as possible in that brief conversation. If they want to make the children happy, they can rejoice their hearts by telling them some fascinating story. They should not assume that children abhor serious and factual subjects: quite to the contrary, children thirst for new and beneficial information, but they want adults to use simple and understandable language in their explanations. Rarely do children avoid listening to serious subjects that are made understandable to them.

Parents and other grown-ups, then, instead of talking nonsense with children, joking, and taking up their time with empty discussions, all the while assuming that the youngsters can pay attention to nothing except frivolous and superficial matters – instead of these, they should explain essential matters to them, using easy-to-understand language and employing many examples. In this way, they will make their children better informed, and instil in them the desire to seek out knowledge, to investigate scientific subjects, and to think and reason logically.

Science has proven that whatever element of the human body remains inactive and unused will little by little cease functioning properly. In the same manner, if the mental faculties are not properly exercised from childhood and are directed only towards the facetious things of life, they will gradually become incapable of manifesting their potential.

This point, therefore, should never be forgotten: improper and inappropriate jesting, when carried beyond moderation and with its only object being to tease, will have detrimental effects on children.

Overlook Trivial Wrongdoings

*Beware lest ye offend the feelings of anyone, or sadden
the heart of any person, or move the tongue in reproach
of and finding fault with anybody, whether he is friend
or stranger . . .*[8]

A serious error some parents commit is the failure to
refrain from browbeating their children for harmless
and trivial wrongdoings which should be overlooked.
Many fathers and mothers seem almost possessed by
an overpowering desire to make their children feel
embarrassed; they derive pleasure from seeing these
most delicate of plants in the divine garden blush for
shame and shed tears. Like a ferocious lion that has
clawed a flagging gazelle and, seeing it powerless,
torments it, such a parent enjoys seeing the feebleness,
helplessness and suffering of their children. This attitude is so heinous that in the name of humanity it
should be rooted out of every family, and parents
should under no condition approach it.

For example, at school, a child has given his fountain-pen to a school friend. An adult doing such a thing
would give himself a pat on the back for his kindness
and generosity, considering that through this meritorious act, he had helped one of his fellow men who was
'down and out'. Some time after this kind-hearted
child has returned home, the mother finds out that
something is amiss, and enquires as to the whereabouts
of the pen. This effectively triggers the child's thinking
process: if he tells the truth, he will most certainly be
scolded; if he does not, it would not be correct from a
moral point of view, for his mother, father and everyone else have taken pains to emphasize for his benefit

that lying is a terrible sin, and that one should never tell lies (even though these same counsellors have told and still tell lies whenever they feel that the situation warrants it).

The child arrives at the decision that he, too, just as a grown-up might do, should now avail himself of a little fib and extricate himself from the indefatigable tongue of his 'unkind' mother, who will otherwise subject him to endless questions. And so, after rapidly considering the options, he tells his mother that he has lost the fountain-pen at school.

Several days later, the mother, through another student, finds out the truth of the matter – that the fountain-pen was given to her son's friend, and that she has been deceived. It is not difficult to picture the next scene, in which the child returns home from school for lunch, and sits at the table with his younger sister and older brother. The mother, like a conqueror who has surprised and captured the fortress of the enemy, turns towards the generous child, and, with a definite glint of joy in her eye, asks, 'What did you tell me a few days ago, when I asked about your pen?' In a flash the child understands what is brewing; he comes to the tragic realization that the game is up, and he cannot even be spared the presence of his brother and sister as he awaits the inevitable tongue-lashing. But, like a prisoner in court, he has no alternative but to sit and listen to the statements of the 'prosecutor' and the decision of the 'judge'. Perturbed, he looks at his mother, but maintains his silence.

The mother, though, persists, repeating her question: 'What did you say happened to your pen?' The child's rejoinder goes like this: 'Oh, Mum. Why make such a big issue out of a pen that is worth so little? I said I lost it at school.'

'Of course a simple pen is not worth discussing,' the mother answers, 'it's your conduct I'm talking about, which is more important than you think. I am asking you what happened to the pen.'

The child again answers, 'I lost it at school.'

'You are telling a lie,' the mother harshly states. 'Own up! You gave it to your friend. How many times have I told you not to do this sort of thing? What did I ever do to deserve a child like you?'

Before the child can open his mouth to defend himself, the mother describes in detail everything that occurred, making him understand that she is aware of it all, and that his struggle is like the struggle of someone drowning at sea.

And so, as a result of his generosity, the child suffers abuse from his 'wise' mother. Ashamed and embarrassed, and in the presence of a sister and brother who make him feel terribly shy, the boy can see no recourse except to weep. With broken heart, weary body, and drooping soul, and deprived of his midday nourishment, he returns to school.

Perhaps, on these occasions, the mother ought to be asked: if the good Lord were to make a tally of *her* trespasses and misdeeds and have her questioned and punished in the same way, what would be her status?

Even the child's hesitation to admit the truth of the incident stems from the parent's ignorance of the subject of training and education, for whenever on similar occasions the child told the truth, he was punished for it.

Such trivial wrongdoings on the part of children should be overlooked, and rectified later on through the use of prudence and foresight, and not by harshness and cruelty. If an archer wants to make a bow from the branch of a tree, and if he throws caution to the winds and bends the bow too rapidly, it will undoubtedly break.

To summarize: it is neither befitting nor praiseworthy to intimidate and embarrass children; rather, fathers and mothers should not lose hold of prudence and caution when dealing with their offspring, but should treat them with the utmost foresight and understanding. If children do wrong, their faults should be rectified as far as possible through scientific and educational means; violent and harsh reactions, extracting confessions and soundly proving fibs and lies should be avoided, because these methods, instead of yielding good results, only lead to worse behaviour.

Beloved educators! Respected mothers and fathers! Your children are like delicate flowers in the vast garden of creation. They need the early-morning breeze and spring rains, not poison-laden winds and frightful storms. Even as the bud that opens with the first stirrings of the dawn breeze, so it is with the child who is not a cord of firewood to be readied with an axe. So do not revile and execrate your children, do not insult and belittle them, do not use force with them, and do not beat, confuse, and embarrass them in front of their peers. Deal with them with the utmost kindness and affection, so that they may revere you from the bottom of their hearts, and perform their duties as children the way God intended.

3

METHODS OF DEALING WITH CHILDREN

*Children are even as a branch that is fresh and green;
they will grow up in whatever way ye train them.*[1]

JUST AS A goldsmith must know the difference between inferior metals and solid gold, and a physician must have studied physiology and the interrelated elements which comprise the human body, and a potter must recognize the various grades of clay, so it is with anyone who determines to undertake the training and education of a child. If he remains unaware of the thoughts, the state, the spiritual and intellectual faculties – in short, the psychology – of the child, he will find himself unequal to the task. Such an educator can be likened to an inexperienced and untrained watchmaker who, instead of repairing a watch, damages it so that it cannot be re-used.

Emerging from our old world of knowledge and perfectionism is a new science which, although still very young, has in one day registered stunning victories in the field of discovery that in the past could not have been achieved in the space of ten years. This is the science of child psychology, which in its brief existence has made exceptional progress in discovering the inner characteristics of children. It has solved many difficult problems, and in so doing has rendered an invaluable service to child training and education.

The Mistake of Treating Children like Grown-ups

From the beginning to the end of his life man passes through certain periods or stages each of which is marked by certain conditions peculiar to itself. For instance during the period of childhood his conditions and requirements are characteristic of that degree of intelligence and capacity.[2]

One of the discoveries of child psychologists is that children, in all aspects, are unlike grown-ups – 'as different as night and day', as the saying goes. The inner faculties of children, including their thoughts and fancies, the scope of their imaginations, their feelings, and the pattern of their reasoning – all differ from those of grown-ups; even their laughing and crying and the way they associate with others differ.

Regrettably, far too often, educators and parents mistakenly regard children as being similar to themselves, and imagine that whatever interests them most probably interests the children too, and that whatever they dislike, the children will dislike, and whatever makes them laugh or fills them with sorrow undoubtedly makes the children laugh or fills them with sorrow also. At every stage and in every matter they make similar comparisons, considering themselves as the standard for the feelings and emotions, the thoughts and opinions, of the children. Such a parent will always find himself and his child facing each other on opposite precipices, with an ever-widening chasm forging itself between these two beings who are so similar in appearance but so dissimilar in nature and behaviour. This mistaken approach gives rise to peculiar developments in the course of a child's training and education, and is more often than not the cause of unpleasant incidents.

Using scientifically-based reasoning and evidence, child psychology has proven that children, at every stage of their lives, possess thought, imagination, feeling, and reasoning capacity which pertain especially to that level of development, and when they move on to the next stage, a definite change occurs in their mentality. Consider, for example, how children of about four or five years old usually imagine that every moving object is alive and has a mind of its own. They attribute a life and a soul to clouds, wind, the moon, the sun, and whatever seems to have movement, just as they do to human beings. They are certain that the moon walks and that the wind flows over the plain just as water does in the river-bed, while the sun crosses the sky at enormous speed.

Parents have, of course, observed that children are delighted by things which do not even bring a smile to the lips of a grown-up. On the other hand, children can become sad and even weep over things which might be quite funny to parents. Many mothers have noticed that, while they are telling a story, their child goes pale and his heart beats fast when he hears a particular description which does not affect the grown-up at all. Imagine that a mother is telling a child the story of 'Beauty and the Beast'. The child interrupts to ask concernedly if the story will have a good or a bad ending, and whether the beast will be hurt or not. When he makes sure that no harm will come to the beast, he takes a deep breath, and with a more relaxed heart, he listens to the rest of the adventure (while still harbouring some doubts in the back of his mind, and repeatedly urging his mother to end the story well).

A child's imagination and his outlook on the world also differ greatly from the imagination and outlook of a grown-up. Think how a child in a big industrialized city stands convinced that a horse's hoof comes from hardwood hammered into shape by a carpenter and securely fastened to the horse's leg with a string, or how something which to us belongs to the realm of impossibility seems easy to the child. You may notice that your child readily believes that the magic horse in the fairy story zooms through the air and the old witch flies up to the heavens riding on her broomstick, while the possessor of forty magic tricks can transform himself into a rock with one gesture, and with another, into a dragon, and with still another, into a bird.

Many parents punish their children for the inappropriateness of their laughter, directing such angry remarks at them as, 'That was not a laughing matter, you little imp,' without realizing that a child cannot help laughing when he sees such trivialities as a cat standing on its hind legs trying to corner a bee, while the bee angers the cat by buzzing around and putting up resistance, or when the shadow of his brother moves across the wall as though it were on a movie screen. He is surprised when his parents do not see the funny side, and he is even more surprised when they make him cry for having laughed.

In short, since these faculties in children differ from their counterparts in grown-ups (both from the physical and spiritual point of view), how can we compare children to ourselves, and judge them according to our own ideas? We should realize that the child cannot comprehend our world, nor can we become like children.

It is clear that every educator (and especially every mother) should be knowledgeable about the psychology of children, and should obtain as much information as possible about a child's make-up so that she can understand deeply and at every level of his growth the way a child thinks, the breadth of his thoughts, imagination and feelings, and upon what principles his demands and inclinations are based. Otherwise, the capacities latent in the child's soul cannot be revealed, and the child's heart remains forever closed in her face.

Children's Demands

*Know that this matter of instruction, of character recti-
fication and refinement, of heartening and encouraging
the child, is of the utmost importance, for such are basic
principles of God.*[3]

How to decide on a reasonable method for handling the requests and demands of children – this is one of the important questions in the field of education.

It should be clear that some types of 'wants' should be accepted by the educator, and other types should be given no consideration whatsoever. Because a young child does not distinguish between good and bad, and because his demands are merely based on spontaneous desire without any foresight, he imagines that whatever he wants should be given him, and whatever wish may cross his childish fancy should be realized. And if he is treated in a way which is contrary to his will, he may become antagonistic towards his dearest and closest acquaintances (even his kind mother), and let loose a flood of resentment.

Many mothers have observed that whenever they do not carry out their children's demands, the child becomes distressed and angry. He shows his anger by crying or whining, by insolence and defiance, or in the form of sob-filled sentences such as 'I don't love you any more,' or 'It seems like you don't love me any more.' and so on. At this point mothers find themselves at their wits' end.

In these and related cases, child psychologists believe that you should treat a child in such a way that, on the one hand, his pride and determination are not wounded and weakened, and on the other hand, you do not let him get carried away by his selfish desires and grow up to be autocratic and dictatorial.

Some parents take one of the two extremes, while only a few choose the path of moderation. That is, some parents (especially mothers), in order to pacify and satisfy the child, provide him with whatever he wants. With a 'Don't worry', they give in to his demands, reasonable or not. In such situations, the child governs his parents and others with whom he comes in contact like an autocratic ruler.

Other parents take exactly the opposite path and reject even the legitimate and logical requests of their child. They treat him angrily, not even listening to what he wants, however logical and sound it may be. With pronouncements such as 'Don't talk,' and, 'Be quiet,' they hurt the sensitive and delicate heart of their child.

To eliminate the two extreme courses of action so

that moderate emotions may prevail, parents (more especially the mother, who is most often at the child's side and the object of his solicitude) have been offered these guidelines:

1. Carefully evaluate the demands of the child and distinguish between those which are reasonable and logical, and those which are unacceptable and harmful.

2. When the distinction between the two categories is clear, the parents should vow – and stick to their vow – not to block any sound, reasonable, and logical demands which the child may have. They should not antagonize him without reason, nor put him under undeserved pressure. Equally important, they should resist with all the power they can muster so as not to give in to inappropriate, unreasonable, or harmful demands, and so as not to be defeated in this battle of wits. In this way the child will gradually but eventually understand that the educator never gives in and bows down to his thoughtless demands, but accepts his sound, useful, and logical requests and carries them out willingly.

If such a method is followed strictly and systematically, and if it is coupled with strong determination, the child will become so accustomed to this pattern that a simple 'no', especially from the mother, will be sufficient to deter him from repeating an unreasonable demand, and the thought of carrying it out will not even occur to him. But if a lack-lustre form of determination hangs over the educator, and if this pattern is neglected, the effect of this guide-line will be entirely effaced. Every educator should always adhere to this point: *give your consent to the reasonable and accept-*

able requests of the child with the utmost kindness and
forbearance, but never submit to his harmful wishes and
demands.

To observe and carry out this guide-line is equally
important from the social aspect, which deserves attention. Since the child will gradually grasp that some
of his wishes and demands are sound, useful, and
acceptable, while others are harmful, improper, and
unreasonable, when he matures, he will naturally ap-
preciate that demands fall into two categories, *worthy*
and *unworthy*, and that the worthy and beneficial
wishes should be translated from thoughts into action,
while the unworthy and harmful demands are not even
to be entertained.

For instance, your nine-year-old tells you with the
utmost simplicity, 'Mummy, my colouring pencils are
finished. Please give me the other ones that you have so
I can do my drawings when my homework is done.'

If you are not concerned with your child's rightful
requests, then without weighing the matter or giving it
any thought, you will immediately say: 'No, it isn't
necessary. Do you want to sharpen and break all your
colouring pencils, and get your hands and clothes
dirty? It's not important that you draw.'

To convince you, the child then says, 'But mother,
the drawings are necessary for school; I must do them.
Isn't that why you bought the colouring pencils?'

But you persist in your point of view and answer,
'Do you think you can break and ruin everything we
buy?'

Finally the child feels utterly powerless, and he asks,
'What shall I do when my homework is finished?'

You answer, 'When you finish your homework, just sit quietly in your place like a grown-up.'

At this stage, in the recesses of his mind, limited by his childish feelings, and according to his understanding and way of thinking, the child believes that he has been treated wrongly. He accuses you of injustice, and in his conscience he finds excuses to disobey your orders. This is because, first of all, the drawings will be asked for at school and he must give an explanation to the teacher. And secondly, the child, according to his natural instinct, cannot do as his mother says and sit quietly and serenely like an adult without doing anything. It is at this point that the child draws up a private strategy to disobey your unjustifiable orders, and sows the seeds of rebelliousness and defiance in his heart at this early age.

Accordingly, if the parents accept the legitimate requests of the child, and reject his improper demands with sound reasoning (which is always acceptable to a child), then he will be convinced (although gradually) that his parents, and especially his kind mother, are his sincere friends and affectionate companions, that they are always his well-wishers, and that whatever is good for him they will agree to, and that whatever is bad, they will reject.

Children as Witnesses

So long as the powers of the mind are various, it is certain that men's judgements and opinions will differ one from another.[4]

Psychologists and researchers have sought to find out exactly how truthful the statements of young children are, and to what extent their sayings can be relied upon and trusted.

Many people believe that children have no ulterior motives and will describe whatever they see or hear without adding a jot or subtracting a tittle, accurately telling the truth of a matter just as they comprehended and evaluated it. Such people always expect the truth from children. This approach, which has been proved incorrect, is the cause of many unfortunate clashes in families; perplexing incidents can stem from the baseless testimonies of children.

We have all seen how carelessness, or failure to heed the principles and fundamentals of education, can lead to differences of opinion between fathers and mothers over unimportant matters, and how these differences little by little become fully-fledged arguments. This eventually leads to a family 'court case', and at the 'trial', whether the judge be the mother or the father, the eye-witnesses almost always include the children. They appear and submit their testimony to the 'court', sometimes willingly and even eagerly, but sometimes out of necessity or by force. In keeping with the opinions of those who regard the statements of children as always true, the judge, whether husband or wife, takes the child's 'evidence' as the criteria for the final decision, fully confident in the child's reliability as a witness. So he bases his own opinion on what the child has said. But the testimony of the child usually springs from his immature imagination, and the parents, because of their mistaken understanding, often fail to observe justice in their judgement and blame the innocent party.

Studies were once conducted by two psychologists, one French, the other German, to examine the testimony of adults, and to see how they are influenced by the power of suggestion and by the power of the imagination. Since Binet (1857–1911) and Stern (1871–1938) published their conclusions and put their writings at the disposal of researchers, other scholars have initiated important experiments dealing with the soundness or falsity of children's testimony, and the relationship they bear to child psychology After careful study, they have reached the conclusion that the statements of children can never be completely relied upon, and their testimony cannot be taken as a valid basis for making decisions. According to various tests which have been carried out, the memories of both adults and children are unable to record accurately the details of situations, very often depicting the principal point of a subject and the truth of an event in a form which but little agrees with what actually happened.

To evaluate the memories of grown-ups and appraise the value of their testimony, Stern did this experiment:

A group of people were given some detailed pictures and drawings and were told to carefully examine them for forty-five seconds; then they were instructed to write down what they had seen. It had been emphasized that those being tested were to be careful and sensible: whatever they wrote had to correspond to reality and had to be reliable to the extent that they could take an oath to the accuracy of their statements. Since their accounts did not agree with the facts, this experiment clearly showed that, no matter how careful and intelligent grown-ups may be, their memories cannot be relied upon.

Similar tests have been given to children, and it has been concluded that their memories are far less reliable than those of grown-ups. One scholar named Lobsen would submit pictures and drawings to selected children. He would then have the children study the material carefully, and write down their observations. On other occasions he would take the children to the theatre, and afterwards would ask them to record what they remembered. After various and frequent tests were conducted, Lobsen arrived at the conclusion that young children are very much influenced by the power of suggestion, and that their statements are vague and careless and do not agree with fact.

Binet conducted a test on elementary school students in Paris. He gave the pupils a piece of cardboard on which were glued a postage stamp, some money, an advertisement, a button, and two photographs – one of a man and one of a group. Each child, tested privately, was asked to look at the items carefully for 12 seconds and then answer questions dealing with colours, shapes, and the way the items were arranged on the cardboard. In addition, he would sometimes give the children misleading questions in order to test the effect of the power of suggestion.

Out of a group of twenty-four pupils, fifteen described the colour of the postage stamp incorrectly. Some students even stated that they had seen the cancellation seal of the post office as well as the name of a city on the stamp, whereas in fact it did not have the seal of the post office. Twenty-one students could not give the position of the button correctly. On the average, out of forty questions which he gave each student, they answered eleven wrong.

Following this, Binet divided the children into groups of three, and questioned each group. It became completely clear to him that the statements given by some children influenced others, while some groups were influenced by the answers of other groups, and would reply accordingly.

An experienced teacher related that one day a young girl told her classroom teacher that she had brought a pen-case with her and had lost it in the school. She insisted that she had left it on a certain bench, and her friends not only backed up her statement, but even pointed out the place on the bench where they last saw it. The following day, the little girl turned up at school carrying the pen-case, and with perfect simplicity told the teacher that it had been at home all along.

Another teacher writes that he once invited a colleague to his classroom to meet his students. The guest spoke to the class for ten minutes without once removing his hat. After his departure, the students were asked in which hand the speaker had been holding his hat. Of the twenty-seven students, seventeen said, 'his right hand,' five said, 'his left hand,' and only five children replied that he had not removed his hat.

A certain teacher asked his students about the colour of the moustache of another teacher whom they all knew well. Ten students replied 'brown,' two 'black,' two 'yellow,' two 'white,' two 'grey,' and one said 'red.' Only one student correctly stated that the teacher concerned had no moustache at all.

These examples help us draw certain conclusions:

1. Children cannot describe events without making alterations or substitutions, for their memories are incapable of recording details accurately. Their statements are often remote from the actual facts.

2. Children are always influenced by personal feelings and the power of suggestion. They mingle their imagination with the actual events, and for this reason their statements can scarcely accord with reality.

3. Sometimes children will become dishonest and purposely alter the facts if it is to their advantage to do so. Hence it cannot be considered prudent to rely on their statements and put confidence in their words and testimonies.

In families, parents should not allow children's suggestions to start an argument, nor to become its focal point. They should instead conduct themselves in such a way that the opportunity for children to make such statements does not arise. If children see estrangement between the father and mother in a situation which involves their testimony, they do not know how to act when they are questioned – for or against which side – nor how to behave in order not to hurt either of the parents.

Since the children are not able to remain completely neutral nor to disentangle themselves from this conflict, they either resort to falsehood compulsively but reluctantly, saying whatever comes to their minds, or they tell the truth, thereby sowing the seed of enmity in the heart of the person against whom they have given testimony. Of course, parents are well aware to what extent this approach corrupts the morals of innocent children, and, in the process, deals a lethal blow to their being and spreads the seeds of discord and disunity in the family.

Children's Questions

They must be constantly encouraged and made eager to gain all the summits of human accomplishment . . .[5]

Let them share in every new and rare and wondrous craft and art.[6]

One inborn trait that the Almighty, in His all-embracing wisdom, has established in man, is curiosity. This intense desire to know has led to the progress and exaltation of mankind, and has been the cause of unravelling many of the world's mysteries, bringing to light profound discoveries and stimulating great inventions.

A young child becomes increasingly inquisitive as he starts speaking and begins to express himself. He wants to understand everything, to comprehend the core of every matter as far as he is able. For this reason, whatever is put within his reach will come under his infantile scrutiny. In order to study the mysteries of a sewing machine, for instance, or to learn the secrets of a clock, he will turn them inside-out, if the absence of other members of the household provides him with the opportunity, and he will analyse and examine them so minutely that they cannot be used again. Mothers become infuriated by such situations, and by the continuous questioning on the part of their children.

If this sense of curiosity, which is inborn and instinctive in young children, is given its due attention by educators, especially mothers, the number of intelligent and knowledgeable youth in the world will surely increase, and the banners of knowledge and learning be raised higher day by day. Educational psychologists have always advised fathers and mothers to answer according to the child's understanding, thoughts, and capacity, and not to be negligent in this all-important matter. They should observe moderation and not lose their tempers when the child insists on, and persists in, understanding the various facets of life, and in comprehending natural phenomena. They should know that questioning is one of the important means whereby children develop understanding and acquire knowledge. How pitiable that some mothers lose their tempers with their innocent children because of their continuous questioning, and so scare the children away, while some fathers pay them no attention at all, believing that they are preventing the children from 'nosiness' and 'rudeness'.

In the same way that a loving mother teaches her precious children how to walk and how to talk – using the utmost patience and forbearance, and losing many nights of sleep so that the child's physical faculties may grow – and just as a loving father bears pain and trouble so that his child may be comfortable, so should they make every effort to perfect the child's mental faculties. Patiently and tolerantly, parents should answer their child's questions and explain the outside world to him as far as possible, using simple words that the child can understand. Above all, they must never deride their children's questions. In their answers, they should not say nonsensical or non-essential things just for fun, nor should they make of their innocent child a source of amusement. All too often grown-ups make children their playthings and break their sensitive and delicate hearts by laughing at their childish expressions.

It once happened that a child noticed an advertisement for cod-liver oil, on which was a picture of a tree – the trade mark of the factory. The child asked, 'Mummy, is this a cod-liver oil tree?' The people around him went so far in their joking and laughing that the poor child ended up crying and fled from the gathering in a state of grief.

When dealing with children, educators should be constantly aware that care, delicacy, politeness and respect are always necessary.

Children's Lies

The hearts of all children are of the utmost purity . . .
They have neither hypocrisy nor deceit.[7]

If lying can be defined as a false statement made deliberately to deceive others, then children, especially those under the age of five, do not actually tell lies. Their statements cannot be labelled lies, even though they may be false. Although grown-ups may think a child is not telling the truth, any deviation from what is truthful is not usually based on bad intentions, nor is it designed to deceive his listeners. If we delve into the causes of making untrue statements, the reasoning behind this argument will be easily understood.

A child sometimes tells lies from fear of punishment or rough treatment, jealousy towards his brothers and sisters, selfishness, or just to show off. Stubbornness, as well, in both words and actions, occasionally leads to lying. If a child tells fibs for any of these reasons, obstinacy may then cause him to cling to his words. But more often than not, a child's story-telling is the product of his imagination. Many parents have noticed that their youngster invents unusual stories, and then tells them as though they had actually happened, with the child himself playing a leading rôle. Because of the intensity of the power of imagination, the gap between fact and fiction is completely erased.

For instance, a child may describe to his mother with the utmost simplicity how he himself was in the pilot's seat of that aeroplane which flew over the house the other evening, or he may claim that on such and such a day, using only his fists and feet, he destroyed the entire wall of the neighbour's house. This should not be interpreted as lying, and the innocent children should not be accused of misbehaviour, nor should they be put under any pressure. The scholar Robert Goup, who wrote a book on children's behavioural patterns, likens punishment of such children to the shooting of harmless doves. At the ages of three and four, children go through a stage in which they are prone to exaggerate, and if this is interpreted as lying, then it is done so unjustly.

Consider, that if you ask a small girl how her doll is, she will happily relate how the little doll cries and screams and disobeys her. If you attempt to ask questions which activate a little boy's imagination, he will tell you many similar stories with characteristic simplicity. From the happy face and the bright eyes of the child it can be clearly understood that he does not regard his words as being anything other than the truth. Thus, on occasion, when a child does something he should not do, unconsciously he puts the blame on others. Rarely does it happen that a child of tender years knowingly and purposely tells lies. Rather, his deviation from propriety has a cause that is not clear to us as grown-ups, but that has to do with his lack of maturity. As the mind matures and gradually grows out of imagination and fancies, this stage of child development will pass. Fibbing on the part of children, therefore, is usually the result of an unbridled imagination, and can never be compared to the lies of grown-ups, which are told for the express purpose of deceiving others.

Jean-Jacques Rousseau believed that lack of proper training may see this trait in children carried through into actual lying, and that if the educator or teacher is not familiar with the psychological make-up of children, he will treat them in such a way that little by little they will feel compelled to tell lies. An important matter which all educators should realize fully is that a child should never be scolded or belittled in such a case, and that he should not be accused of lying in the presence of friends and peers. In other words, an issue should not be made of it. Even more important is that educators should not strike or punish a child for having deviated from the path of truth. On the contrary, with the utmost patience and kindness they should gradually correct this condition, fully aware that this is a characteristic of childhood which will eventually be outgrown.

Sometimes the educator thinks that by inflicting punishment he can correct the condition immediately and so guide the child to truthfulness (in the adults' estimation). But the end result will be exactly the opposite, since the child by nature is involuntarily under the influence of his own imagination. Being punished will be of little avail in the face of the conditioning of nature. To protect and save himself from the cruelty of the uninformed educator, he will cling to bad conduct and to actual lying, and little by little he will have so much practice in it that he will become an accomplished liar of the first degree.

To clarify the matter, we will give an example: Your seven-year-old returns from school with bright eyes and a beaming face and joyfully tells you that today at school he knew his lesson better than the others and was greatly admired by the teacher; the rest of the pupils were told to follow his example, and the instructor told them to go to him and congratulate him. The story continues that one of the students felt jealous and began crying; during recess that same person picked on him and even went so far as to beat him up. Then the principal came to sort things out, and so forth . . .

Knowing your child as you do, you do not think that he has progressed to such an extent as to have become the sole focus of the teacher's admiration. But if you are not careful, you try to expose your child by angrily saying, 'All these stories are nonsense,' and 'You should be ashamed of yourself,' or 'Get up this very minute and we'll pay a visit to your teacher to see whether your nonsense is true or not, if you have told lies you'll never hear the end of it!' Then the unfortunate child, like a drunkard becoming sober, returns to his natural state and deeply regrets his poetical fancies which he himself had actually believed. Thinking of his parents' punishment and imagining himself being belittled at school, he starts to tell other surprising stories so as to protect himself. Countless times he claims, while crossing his heart and hoping to die if what he has said is false, that if mother carries through her plan to look into the matter at school, they will expel him, all the other children will mistreat him, whatever he has said was the truth, the child who fought with him would think the mother was coming to punish him, and so on. So many falsehoods emerge that the situation becomes impossible to deal with, and the outcome will be contrary to the one desired.

If, however, you are careful enough to say nothing to the child at that time, not even to react happily to his inventions, and if you just listen quietly and serenely, after a while the influence of the child's imagination will wear off. He will either forget his story entirely, or will confess to his mother that it was a joke. Or he may think that the story was a figment of his imagination, related only to himself, from which he has derived some immediate pleaure. At this juncture the mother can very wisely and kindly counsel her child and tell him that, God willing, he will study in such a way that what he has said as a joke will become reality, that others will follow his example, and the teacher will admire him. It is even possible for the mother to say to him that he has foretold his future, and that she hopes everything will turn out as he described. If the circumstances are suitable, she can prudently explain that whatever story a child tells should be as it actually happened.

In short, this matter is both important and delicate, and grown-ups are dealing with sensitive, tender, and imaginative creatures whose hearts are more delicate than water-lilies and will break with the slightest of careless acts. If, on the other hand, the child is left to himself, he will not, of course, be corrected. For this

reason the educator should guide the child with concentrated attention, and with the utmost patience and
kindness. Rather than employing force and threats, she
should try to follow the guidance of child psychology.

Selfishness in Children

For self-love is kneaded into the very clay of man . . .[8]

*If man be imbued with all good qualities but be selfish, all
the other virtues will fade or pass away . . .*[9]

The love that each person has for himself impels him to
protect and safeguard his own being as far as possible,
and to do things which benefit his own person while
avoiding anything repugnant and harmful; this love,
bequeathed to us by the Almighty, clearly serves to
perpetuate the human race.

If this instinctive love for oneself is kept within the
bounds of moderation, then it is praiseworthy and
useful; but if, God forbid, it is carried to extremes, and
develops along egotistical and selfish lines, a great deal
of harm will result. Many and diverse are the precious
gems of knowledge given us in literature by great
writers and scholars testifying to the baseness of selfish
behaviour.

In children, the instinct of self-love is very intense,
and in very young children, self-interest and the avoidance of displeasure are the pivots of their thought
process: they want everything for themselves, and see
the world through the portal of their own pleasure;
they see themselves as the centre of attention, and
imagine that the world and whatever is in it were
created for them, and that everyone should serve and
obey them.

Many of the actions and words of young children mean little to grown-ups, but even though they may seem strange to us, they seem quite clear and logical to the children themselves, for their impulses during this period of life are mostly instinctive. When, for instance, a child wants to eat something sweet and sees that his mother has put candies and cookies in the cupboard, he unhesitatingly pries open the cupboard door and eats whatever he wants, unaware that the parents have different plans for these goodies, and consider such actions by the 'headstrong' child improper and deserving of punishment. Or, perhaps, a little girl notices that her doll needs a new dress. Without hesitation, she gets hold of whatever material her mother may have – even if it is brocade – and cuts it up to make a dress for the doll. When the mother discovers what is afoot, and, infuriated, screams at the child and asks how she could do such a thing, the girl, with complete frankness, replies: 'I needed it.' Then she considers whether or not there is a more convincing statement she could have made, and says to herself, 'I needed it, so I took it.'

The principal task of educators in this matter is to attempt to channel this swift-flowing flood into its correct course, and not permit 'love of self' to develop into self-centred behaviour. To realize this goal, however, certain points must be carefully observed:

1. It is essential that children be repeatedly and wisely reminded that there are others, too, who deserve to benefit from the many things which an All-loving Creator has provided for our use, and that each member of a family should concern himself with the others,

should serve and help one another, and always show consideration.

2. The Golden Rule, 'Don't wish for others what you wouldn't wish for yourself', should be repeated and, in different forms, depicted for the children, so that they may see it put into action. The children should be reminded of this important moral point every time the opportunity to do so presents itself, but this should be done very carefully.

3. More important than anything else is that parents should do nothing to fan the flames of this fire of self-love which burns within a child. That is, they should not admire him undeservedly, and should avoid trumpeting such observations as 'This child of ours is really unique. You wouldn't believe how good he is – and everything he does is so cute! Look how strong and healthy he is. And his smile is so sweet!' In other words, they should not be like a mother deer doting on her fawn, for inappropriate praise and admiration of a child leads him into complacency and pride, and can ruin his morals and behaviour.

A wise parent can recognize when to encourage, admire and praise his child, so that each child learns from an early age that every action has its own reward or punishment, and that if he does something praiseworthy, he will be rewarded, and if he does something blameworthy, he will be punished. If from their childhood years children discover that reward and punishment are an inseparable part of society, they will little by little rectify their conduct. Encouragement and expressions of appreciation should not be confused with unwarranted admiration, for good acts merit ap-

preciation, while exaggerated praise and excessive admiration are both blameworthy and harmful.

If you encounter selfish and egotistical individuals
in society – and regrettably such people are not few in
number – and if they make trouble, or are the cause of
the inefficient operation of many institutions, then you
can be certain that the chief reason for their behaviour
is the lack of attention given to this important subject
by mothers and fathers who have been negligent in
training their offspring, and have left these tender
saplings to be straightened either by fire or the axe.

4

SOME COMMON PROBLEMS

*Every child is potentially the light of the world – and at
the same time its darkness; wherefore must the question
of education be accounted as of primary importance.*[1]

*The root cause of wrongdoing is ignorance, and we
must therefore hold fast to the tools of perception and
knowledge. Good character must be taught.*[2]

YOUNG CHILDREN, in general, are ruled by their instincts. Their actions are based on natural stimuli, and
rarely stem from the power of mind and thought. Since
these powers are not yet properly developed in children, they spontaneously try to obtain whatever they
desire and whatever pleases them, and do not think a
matter through. The qualities of foresight and prudence, and the ability to distinguish between good and
bad, are unattainable for children. For this reason,
they often perform actions which seem very unusual to
the parents.

'Stubbornness'

*Man reacheth perfection through good deeds, voluntarily
performed, not through good deeds the doing of which
was forced upon him.*[3]

A child cannot resist playing with the water in a nearby
pond; in his state of joy, it never occurs to him that he
might fall in and drown. Or he may excitedly use as

toys such items as razors, knives, scissors, or needles, without giving so much as a thought to the danger involved. When the mother tries to separate him from these playthings he resists strongly, because such desires are instinctive to the child. Sometimes the situation deteriorates to the degree that the impatient mother, in order to protect her inexperienced child from danger, resorts to punishment. The child intensifies his resistance and begins to cry, considering his mother the enemy of his happiness, recreation and comfort. If these restraints and prohibitions continue, the child becomes disobedient and rebellious; he will act discourteously and talk back to his mother.

This state of resistance is often referred to as 'stubbornness' by mothers who call their children 'headstrong' and 'obstinate'. In order to rectify the child's conduct, the mother often strikes or vilifies him, or uses other kinds of force – all of which have the effect of increasing the stubbornness and corrupting the morals of their offspring.

Incidents resembling the following have often occurred: A mother forcibly takes a knife from her child's hands and proceeds to hide it, telling him not to play with such things. But after a few minutes have passed, she finds the child playing with the knife again. She shouts at him: 'Put that knife down! How many times must I tell you not to play with such things?' The child, who is totally fed up with being told what to do and what not to do, tells his mother, clearly and without any embarrassment, 'If I want to play, it's none of your business. Leave me alone and go and mind your own business.' Punishment of the child is the final outcome of these arguments, but eventually spanking and abuse lose their effect; as the plot thickens, the father is obliged to interfere. The harmful consequences of these encounters and conflicts are clear to everyone.

In order to prevent the 'obstinacy' of children, many scientific and practical methods can be used which may solve this problem without having to resort to violent means:

1. Young children, by nature, cannot sit still for long; their latent abilities must develop from childhood, and their limbs must become strong through exercise, gymnastics and movement. Mothers who want their children to sit idle and still in a corner act contrary to the God-given nature of the child, and face an impossible task in attempting to put this concept into practice. Children should not, therefore, be prevented from playing and moving around. A few toys and playthings suffice to busy them. Every father and mother, if they but think a little about the matter, can provide children with toys suitable to their ages and interests and according to the limitations of the family finances. Nor do the toys have to be expensive ones: simple pieces of wood and boards, a few pieces of paper, some pencils, boxes, home-made dolls, and similar items can keep the children occupied.

2. When children are involved in some dangerous action, parents should immediately distract them by showing them more interesting things to do rather than taking forcible measures. For instance, if a child is holding on to a razor, instead of expressing feelings of fright and shock, and making the child cry and become more 'stubborn' by wrenching the razor from

his hand, the parent should immediately interest the child in something else. A candy or a coloured ball, for example, can distract the child from what he is playing with.

3. If a child is busy doing harmless things, then the mother should do nothing to stop him. If he is occupying himself by tearing up waste paper on the rug, for instance, and the only harmful result is that the room must be re-swept, then the mother should not mind the trouble, nor prevent the child from playing in this way. Extreme strictness, and always being on his back with inappropriate regulations and restraints makes a child nervous and then rebellious, causing him to put up resistance even though he knows better. Many children have told me that they regard their mothers as disturbers of their tranquillity and even as their enemies. They say such things as, 'My mother is never on my side.' 'Everything I do, she stops me.' 'My mother is my enemy and doesn't want to see me happy.' 'I don't feel wanted in the house.' If this feeling of hatred increases, and the child harbours a negative attitude towards his mother, then the task of training will be very difficult, and fraught with dangerous consequences for the child.

4. · Children by their very nature need to take walks in fresh air, to go on outings, and enjoy suitable recreation. Fathers and mothers should not deprive their children of the bounty of their company, and should take them for walks and outings in clean surroundings. When a child grows naturally and does not become disheartened because of a suffocating environment, and if he is not subjected to unreasonable restrictions and regulations imposed by the mother, nor

deterred from harmless games and suitable recreation, then he will not manifest stubbornness, and will not resort to throwing tantrums.

Secretive Behaviour

The child when born is far from being perfect. It is not only helpless, but actually is imperfect, and even is naturally inclined towards evil. He should be trained, his natural inclinations harmonized, adjusted and controlled, and if necessary suppressed or regulated, so as to ensure his healthy physical and moral development.[4]

Mothers can often be heard complaining that their children do things in a stealthy way around the house. They are convinced that harm both for the family and for the children themselves will be the eventual result. Clearly, they have no patience with these secretive acts, but at the same time, they confess their inability to rectify the situation.

Most young children do involve themselves in secretive acts; they exert the utmost effort to conceal many of their everyday actions from the mother, and to carry out their deeds without being disturbed by anyone. Before trying to correct this behaviour, the educator must first familiarize himself with the underlying causes of it, so that he can rectify it better and easier.

It is the author's proffered opinion that the secretive acts of children can be explained in this manner: because of their natural instincts, young children intensely and greedily try to acquire everything which interests them – namely, anything which stimulates any of the five senses and leads to pleasure, or anything which kindles their sense of curiosity. They choose any means which they find suitable to realize their goal and so they very often neglect those moral principles which are accorded a high position by adults and are not open to question. Here are two examples to clarify the point.

I. A young child is sitting near the table and has his eyes fixed on different kinds of fruit. Their aroma, colour and taste strongly tempt him. Immediately his instinct issues instructions and orders, and his stimulated nerves are set in motion. An inner voice tells him, 'Stretch out your hand and take that nice, red, juicy apple and enjoy eating it.'

The mother, for her part, has repeatedly instilled this advice into him: 'My dear child – please don't touch the fruit. The table is being set for the guests. Be careful not to take anything. Children mustn't touch something which is for guests.'

At this juncture the unfortunate child is faced with two conflicting issues: from one side, an overpowering appetite for fruit troubles him; from the other side, fear of the mother torments him. A battle ensues between these two forces, and out of all this, natural inclination and innate desire often dominate motherly warnings. Worded differently, he is 'tempted by the devil'. But his God-given intelligence finally arrives at a solution to this intricate problem, and quietly and convincingly instructs him in this way: 'My little child – so eager to eat the fruit, so crazy about those lovely apples, mouth-watering cherries, and appetizing apricots, but so afraid to take them openly because of your mother. Well then, it will be best to take them when your mother is not looking; that way, both goals will be attained: you will have the delicious fruit, and your mother will be none the wiser.'

After this clarifier has been issued, the child leaves his seat in such a way that the mother never notices his absence. He approaches the bags of fruit which have just been brought from the market, and selects whatever fruit appeals to him. Quickly, and demonstrating superb skill, he hides himself – perhaps in an out-of-the-way corner behind the kitchen table – and hurriedly disposes of the evidence; wiping his lips, he returns to his mother and pretends that her advice has had its intended effect on him, and that he has not even glanced at the fruit on the table. As a reward for this 'trustworthiness' and 'goodness', he is even praised by his mother. When, however, she goes to the bags of fruit and notices that they have been tampered with, she directs her suspicions at the cleaning lady or helper, and her shouts resound throughout the house. The 'meek and innocent' child watches the drama from a vantage point in a corner, but does not own up to his wrongdoing because he does not regard himself as the person at fault, for he says to himself, 'I felt like eating the fruit, and so I did. If my mother prefers strangers and guests to me, her child, and keeps the fruit for them, then she, the unkind mother, is to be blamed, and not I, a small child with a strong craving for fresh fruit.'

2. Every single day a child comes across things in the home which attract his attention, and, like a person possessed, he determines to unravel their mysteries. He is hasty and greedy, and nourishes the desire to become tiny enough to enter an apparatus by way of one of its

very small openings, and discover its hidden secrets. He has noticed, for instance, that at regular intervals the wall clock chimes, and gives the correct time with an harmonious sound like that of a musical instrument. The curious child sets about trying to understand this oddity. Aware as he is that it is absolutely forbidden to touch the clock, he draws up a plan to remove it, using the same skill as before. The absence of other members of the household provides him with the hoped-for opportunity. Straightaway he goes to the wall clock, raises himself by climbing on a stool, and manages somehow to remove the time-piece from its place. Heaven knows what will happen to the clock and to the aspiring young child.

Briefly stated, the principal reason underlying the stealthy acts of children – be it their intense desire for eating or their all-consuming interest in discovering how things work, or anything else – is enjoyment. We will not dwell on the observation that adults too are under the influence of this same principle, and were it not for moral and religious codes and considerations, their condition would be similar to that of children. Rather, it will serve our purpose in this book to give two methods which are useful in preventing secretive behaviour in children.

1. If her financial state permits, the mother should avoid having her children develop 'hungry eyes'; nor should she give her approval to have everything put under lock and key. That is to say, the mother should, according to the family's financial capability, give the child adequate nourishment, while bearing in mind the rules of health and hygiene. The child should receive

sufficient food, fruit and so forth, so that his basic requirements are met, and his gaze is not directed towards other people's hands or towards the closed cupboards which are chock-full of edibles that have not been shared with the child, but are being kept for emergencies and visitors. Put in another way, whatever is purchased and brought home, whether food, drink, or clothes, the child, according to his God-given right, should receive his portion.

Nothing should be kept hidden or concealed, because stealthiness in the actions of the mother leads to stealthy acts by the child. This stealth is completely contagious: it goes from grown-ups to children. When, for instance, some fruit is brought into the home, the mother should give the child his share, making sure he understands that he has had his portion, and that the rest, which is put with the child's knowledge in a specific place, is for others. The custom of placing such things under lock and key should be done away with. The mother should, however, keep an unobtrusive eye on the child so that she can counsel him indirectly and prudently if he transgresses.

Suppose that a child goes to the cupboard and takes cookies and fruit in excess of his own share. He should not be made the recipient of a harsh and severe reaction from the mother. Toleration is necessary as the first step, and later, at an appropriate time, he can be fully reminded and admonished. An ancient Arabic saying goes: 'Whenever something is forbidden, man's desire cannot be hidden.' As soon as the child notices that no harsh restrictions are imposed upon his eating habits, that no injustice has been levelled against him, that the cupboards remain unlocked, and that if he feels like taking something to eat he will not be scolded, reproached, vilified, or struck, then gradually 'his eyes will be as satisfied as his stomach', and his greed for sneaking food will become a thing of the past.

2. So as to satisfy the child's burning curiosity, he should to some extent be informed of the intricacies of those things which are exciting and fascinating to him. Also, means should be provided for him to find out how these mysterious things work. For example, the parents can buy an inexpensive clock and leave it at the disposal of the child so that, when he wants to see for himself how it works, he can handle it as he likes. In this way, his curiosity will be appeased, and his greed and acute desire will little by little lessen.

The two above-mentioned examples, together with the two methods which followed, are given only as samples so that parents, from this brief explanation and by relying on their God-given intelligence, common sense, and accumulated experience, can take steps to discover further ways as needed to prevent secretive behaviour in their children.

Jealousy and Rivalry

Be fair to yourselves and to others, that the evidences of justice may be revealed, through your deeds, among Our faithful servants.[5]

The integrity of the family bond must be constantly considered, and the rights of the individual members must not be transgressed . . . Just as the son has certain obligations to his father, the father likewise has certain obligations to his son.[6]

Children in many families find themselves pitted

against each other in competition. They regularly experience deep feelings of jealousy towards one another. As a result, struggles and rivalry continuously abound: if a mother makes a dress for her older daughter, the younger one insists that one be made for her too, even though she may already have many; if a father purchases a pair of shoes for his younger son, the older one expects the same treatment.

You may have observed, for instance, that the children fix their eyes on their mother whenever she divides candy or fruit among them, ever watchful lest one of them receive a little extra or a little less. Even after the children receive their shares, they compare, count, measure or weigh them to make sure that in the distribution they have not lost out, and that 'justice' has been done.

If by justice we mean the administration of rights to all those who have a just claim, with due consideration given to rank, age, intellectual capacity, and other virtues, then its meaning differs from that commonly understood by children, who demand completely equal treatment. For this reason, they do appear to be selfish and egotistical; considering their demands and inclinations as the only standard, the children judge everything from a personal point of view.

The reason for this egoism is also quite clear: during childhood, children are governed by natural instinct, and common sense and the faculty of reasoning have yet to manifest themselves. If used properly, as in the acquisition of knowledge and virtues, for instance, rivalry and competition are acceptable. But if jealousy becomes the cause of hatred and enmity among children, and if, within a family, it arouses suspicion and distrust and gives rise to arguments, then it is unquestionably very harmful and dangerous. As grownups, these children will be characterized by selfishness, a self-centred attitude, and cold-heartedness.

The two methods which follow are given for the purpose of preventing such harmful rivalry:

1. Discrimination on the part of the parents towards their offspring – through showing intense love and affection towards one child while paying scant attention towards another – is the greatest single cause of jealousy and unhealthy rivalry among children. It has often been witnessed how a parent will single out one of the children and call him his 'favourite', and will confer excessive attention on him at the expense of the others. As a direct result of this inconsiderate approach, feelings of jealousy and competition build up in the other children, and these gradually give way to outright hatred and enmity.

For example, the father of a family returns home and, without paying the least bit of attention to his other children, goes directly towards his pet child, hugs him, kisses and pampers him, and gives him the gifts he has bought; in the opinion of the other children, he is totally spoiling the child. If an impartial and observant person is present at this time, he will deduce from the faces of the children the feelings of repulsion which they harbour as a result of their father's unfair action. Clearly, such reprehensible behaviour will naturally ignite the fires of jealousy and discontent in the hearts of the children, generating attitudes of rivalry towards each other.

The parents should pay due attention to all the children as befits their age and position in the family, and should, moreover, praise their abilities and understanding, and encourage the development of talents and perception. They should frequently ask about their condition, and should observe complete justice in the family, taking care not to trample on the rights of any child; in this way the children will recognize that their station is fully preserved within the family, and discrimination is non-existent.

The father and mother are like a governing body to the family, and the children, its subjects with equal rights. In the same way that a just government respects the rank of each of its citizens and deals with everyone equally, so it is with parents, who should treat their children in this same fashion within the boundaries of their small and limited 'country': they should not favour one over another, but should shower love and compassion on all the children, and should take adequate precautions to protect the rank and station of each one of them.

2. Parents, whenever appropriate, and through the use of proverbs and stories related in simple language, should bring their children to understand that each one of them has a different station in the family according to age, perception, ability, and knowledge, and that all the children cannot be placed on the same footing nor treated in the same manner. It is necessary, for instance, to give more food to one's elder son because his height, weight and natural requirements for nourishment are greater than those of his younger brother. In return, the elder brother is capable of doing certain types of work which the younger brother cannot. If, for example, wood is needed to fuel the

fireplace, the elder of the two is asked to gather it, while the smaller brother is not expected to carry out this difficult task.

The goal is this: the parents should explain completely and in a kind and loving manner the duties and station of all their children, and help them to understand that, as God is kind to all His servants in spite of each member of society having a specific station and duty, so it is that they love each and every one of the children equally and from the bottom of their hearts, and although all of them are dear and precious, they cannot all be treated in the same way, inasmuch as their ages, capacities, perceptive abilities, level of knowledge, and types of experience differ, and, of course, their duties are not of the same calibre. Jealousy and rivalry of children within the family will surely be minimized if parents give this subject their whole-hearted attention.

Dealing with Tale-bearers

For the tongue is a smouldering fire, and excess of speech a deadly poison. Material fire consumeth the body, whereas the fire of the tongue consumeth both heart and soul.[7]

All the Divine Educators have condemned the practice of backbiting, and have advised their followers against it in no uncertain terms (see Chapter 8). The present writer does not wish to deal directly with the subject here, for every well-informed person is fully aware that backbiting is a despicable action; instead, the causes of backbiting will be explored, and ways will be suggested to prevent this contemptible habit from becoming established in children.

Anyone who has dealt with or associated with young children has observed that they nourish an ardent desire to be 'bearers of news'. In general, they are inclined to relate to others what they have seen or heard in an excited and exaggerated fashion. Consider, for example, this exchange between two sisters, one thirteen, the other, seven years old: as the elder of the two is returning home from school, the younger one, with bright eyes, flushed cheeks, and throbbing heart, rushes to greet her and tell her what she has seen and heard – that father and mother said such-and-such about her and disgraced her, or that she accidently ran into one of her sister's friends, who reported that she, the elder sister, had received low marks, that the teacher had punished her, and so on.

If any obstacles stand in the way, or if the child minds her parents, she will carry out this deed in secrecy. For instance, in the interval that her mother is out of the room, the child will relay the information to the other party in a flash.

This condition – the burning desire to be a 'news bearer' – is present in almost all children. Their objective is not, of course, backbiting in the real sense of the word; neither is their purpose misrepresentation, denigration, or slander; it is childrens' natural impulse to relate what they see and hear, because these sights seem very strange and noteworthy to them.

If this tendency in children is not rectified, then little by little backbiting, slander, and tale-bearing become habitual: as grown-ups, they will find it extremely difficult to curtail these habits.

Certain methods have been proposed to prevent the establishment of this practice:

1. Parents (and particularly the mother), should counsel the children with tender words and happy faces, and divert them from this blameworthy action. They should, moreover, by using examples and stories, depict the repulsiveness of this habit, making them understand that anything which gives offence or causes grief should not be said. More particularly, they should show the children that since they themselves are hurt and displeased if someone brings them bad news, then naturally, if they give bad news to someone else, that person will also be hurt and saddened. In short, the mother and father, using the most suitable language, and at appropriate times, should divert their children from tale-bearing and speaking ill of others.

2. Parents should forbid backbiting and tale-telling in families, making their children understand that they loathe this terrible deed, and that they never want their children to speak ill of others or find fault with them. To attain this objective, the parents should exercise extreme caution so as not to disparage others, nor to backbite, while in the presence of their offspring. The moment children begin speaking in this manner, the parents should firmly but calmly tell them to change the subject, and point out that only the good qualities in people should be mentioned, for backbiting is sinful, and is not permitted in the family. In other words, parents themselves should not backbite, nor should they allow their children to step into this arena.

3. In some families where the parents are not familiar with the principles of education, they actually

drive their children towards backbiting and tale-telling. Consider this example:

A mother instructs her little child to listen carefully to his father, and to report to her immediately if he hears anything said about the mother when she is not present. When the opportunity arises, the mother asks the child if his father has said anything about her. Then the bird of the child's imagination takes flight and soars so high that whatever comes into his mind emerges in his words. The mother, relying on the mistaken idea that unadulterated truth comes from a child's lips, firmly establishes a hatred towards the father in her heart, and sets about taking revenge – all because of the baseless utterances and daydreams of the young child.

This method should never be experimented with in families, but should be dispensed with altogether. Never should the father and mother lead their children towards gossipy and frivolous discussions. In this way, to some extent it will be possible to curtail the spread of backbiting in society.

Spoilt Children

Whoso cleaveth to justice, can under no circumstances, transgress the limits of moderation.[8]

The relationship between parents and children tends to one of these two extremes:

The first group includes those parents in whose presence young children are as lifeless as pictures on the wall, for such is the degree of their submissiveness that they dare not speak. In these families the parents even disregard the reasonable requests of the children, treat them roughly and harshly, and deprive them of most of their rights. Authoritarian measures and unfairness prevail to such a degree that the parents and other members of the household can laugh loudly and joke, but any attempt by the children to emulate their example will meet with punishment. This is particularly applicable in the presence of guests, at which time the youngsters are expected to sit statue-like and obey to the letter the dictates of 'politeness' and 'dignity', shunning any activity which belittles them in the sight of others.

In the second category are those parents who give their children absolute freedom, leaving them completely to themselves and avoiding all instructions, whys and wherefores. These people are of the belief that children should enjoy freedom during the childhood years, behaving as they like until the age of maturity when the light of intelligence will cause them to distinguish good from bad, and they will automatically shun every blameworthy act. Children often become spoilt and unruly in these families; their childhood – those precious years during which they are supposed to acquire befitting characteristics and develop praiseworthy habits – wastes away, and as adults, they find themselves afflicted with countless hardships.

Picture, for example, a five-year-old child surrounded by friends and relatives who are showering him with affection. No sooner is the child put down by the mother than the father picks him up; before he finishes cuddling him, someone else takes him in his arms; then a fourth person props the child on his knees, and later on somebody hugs him, and so it continues.

When that 'precious' child frees himself from the clutches of his friends and relatives, he starts tearing around the room, throwing himself from one corner to another. If there are any fruits or other edibles spread out on the table, he grabs them, in the midst of his leaping and tumbling, and bolts them down in a gluttonous fashion; if he eats peanuts, the shells will soon be scattered over the floor. Perhaps he will spot his grandfather's walking-stick next, and he will scurry around poking at things and lifting up shirt collars. Then it occurs to him to give his elder sister a solid rap on the head in order to 'discipline' her . . .

Praise for the agility and nimbleness of the child can be heard from all sides, and his unrestrained activities are watched by shining eyes and smiling faces. If the mother wishes to admonish the child and divert him from his rough and tumble, the others rapidly raise objections and say, 'Don't let it bother you – he is only a child.' 'Weren't you a child once? Leave him to himself . . .' Then they turn to the child and say, 'Go and play, little boy – we told your mother not to worry about what you do.' 'Run along – but be careful not to trip and fall.' It is not difficult to assess the behaviour which this spoiled child will manifest in later years.

When a child grows up in such an unrestrained manner, he will never obey his parents, and from dawn until dusk the slightest provocation causes him to throw tantrum after tantrum. The mother may say, 'Darling, go and wash your hands and face before you sit down to breakfast.' But the headstrong child ignores this instruction and starts eating. When the mother repeats her plea, the child answers, 'No, no, no! I don't want to. It's none of your business if I want to eat breakfast with dirty hands.' And if the mother tries to force the child to obey her, she is greeted with such an outburst of screaming and kicking that day itself is turned into night. The mother, reduced to a state of powerlessness, sees no alternative but to give in to the child and leave him to himself.

Both of these approaches are detrimental and dangerous to children. Parents should use moderation, because undue strictness and harshness, authoritarianism, and ignoring all the rights of young children, are just as damaging as unbridled and excessive freedom.

People generally grow up over-shy and easily disillusioned, if, as children, they experienced excessive pressure and inner torment; they always feel deprived of their rights, and their level of activity is unusally low. On the other hand, spoilt and unrestrained children, upon attaining adulthood, tend to be egotistical, self-complacent, and shirkers of rules and duties. Imposing their opinions on others and ignoring sound advice characterize their everyday actions, as they see the world and its people only through their own eyes.

It is evident that both these parent-child relationships should, as far as possible, be avoided, and that parents and educators should adhere to moderation in the training and education of their children. This will lead to a decrease in the number of extremist elements in society, and will permit felicity and prosperity to make their marks on the assemblage of mankind.

Temper Tantrums

We also observe in infants the signs of aggression and lawlessness, and that if a child is deprived of a teacher's instructions his undesirable qualities increase from one moment to the next.[9]

Most young children have temper tantrums at one stage or another, and mothers faced with this form of misbehaviour encounter innumerable difficulties as they attempt to apply different solutions to this intricate problem.

A child may start crying for no obvious reason. A steady stream of tears runs down his cheeks. If this fails to get the attention of his mother, and if nobody fondles him, the crying and fidgeting intensify. Like someone seized by nervous convulsions, he stamps his feet on the floor, bashes his head against the wall, and throws aside anything in his path – screaming hysterically all the while. The anxious mother first tries to quieten the child; gently and kindly she asks several times, 'Why are you screaming, darling? Won't you tell me what has happened?' But the kindness and consideration of the mother only serve to intensify his yelling. For a while, he prances around like a chicken with its head cut off, but eventually the mother's persistence pays off, and he begins talking. He asks for some fruit. 'Darling, you know that we don't have any fruit in the house,' the mother says, 'wait until your father comes home and then we will buy some.' Knowing full well that the mother is unable to get any fruit immediately, the child continues to insist that he wants some. When this leads nowhere, his demands turn to another unattainable matter. Finally he has his mother 'climbing up the wall', and the matter comes to a swift conclusion with the child being struck and punished.

A mother once related this occurrence to me: 'In the middle of a warm summer night my eight-year-old child woke up and asked for some water. When I brought him a glass of water, he asked me if it was from the tap or from the fridge. I told him, "It's from the tap. Drink it, and don't talk much or you will have bad dreams." This answer unloosed an outburst of criticism, and the child said, "This water is warm. I want cold water." I had to fill the glass with cold water and bring it back to him. But his lips had no sooner touched the glass than he screamed, "Why is this water so cold? What kind of water is this supposed to be?" I said, "The water is from the refrigerator. Didn't you tell me you wanted cold water?" The child angrily answered, "I don't want this water. It is tasteless."
Anyway, he refused to drink the water, and, to make a long story short, I became very frustrated because of having to reason the situation out with him, and he went back to sleep angry and in tears.'

It is not unusual to find such children in families. One has a temper tantrum because of a problem of clothes, another because of food; the father's statements offend a third child, while a fourth regards some comment made by the mother as unbearable. In short, each one, for different reasons, experiences these emotional outbursts, and the parents – more often than not, the mothers – become deeply tormented and suffer many nerve-racking moments.

This type of misbehaviour in children is usually

based on one of the following reasons:

1. Weak and feeble children, and children with nutritional deficiencies, who are always in an irritable state, whine and throw tantrums more often and more quickly than do other children. They are over-sensitive, easily offended, quick to anger, and cannot tolerate the smallest amount of harshness. Since they do not have the strength to endure hardship, it requires very little provocation to cause them to misbehave. Briefly, the cause of repeated temper tantrums in many children can be traced to chronic physical trouble, ill-health, and frayed nerves.

2. If parents bring up their children as selfish, spoilt, pampered, and egotistical individuals; if they give in to all their unreasonable demands; if they immediately provide them with whatever they want; then naturally the children will have temper tantrums. At every moment they come up with a new demand; they rule and enslave their parents, and drape the chains of captivity around their necks.

It requires a major and scientifically-sound effort to reduce the severity of children's temper tantrums and eliminate their causes. Here are two methods which should help parents.

1. Children whose health is impaired and who have nervous disorders should be taken to competent specialists and treated. Relief from their ailments will leave them much more relaxed and much more tranquil. No one should annoy or anger them in the home: as far as possible, whatever aggravates and irritates a weak and sensitive child should be avoided.

These children are, of course, more in need of medical treatment than of punishment and discipline; their temper tantrums cannot be got rid of by firmness.

Many parents have lost children out of sheer negligence, and afterwards have drowned themselves in an ocean of tears. An infection should be treated before it spreads and worsens, and in this important matter there should be no indecision or hesitancy.

2. From the first, parents should not give in to the illogical demands of their children, neither should they allow their patience to wear thin. On the contrary, they should be so firm and staunch that the children will gradually come to realize that many demands would, if met, prove to be harmful, and that it is necessary for them to dispense with some of their wishes.

A child who does not learn to exercise control over his demands is like a car without its steering wheel. When a child, as a result of insight and experience, arrives at the discovery that no matter how much he cries and screams, the parents will never bow down to those demands which are nonsensical and harmful, then he will pause to assess what the outcome of another tantrum may be, and will dispense with this form of behaviour, sparing both himself and others the pain and torment involved.

If, after observing the above-mentioned methods, parents see that their children still do not bring their temper tantrums under control, they should consult child psychologists and make use of their guidance. Various chronic ailments and mental disturbances are the primary causes of persistent misbehaviour of this type.

Inactive Children

Therefore must the mentor be a doctor as well: that is, he must, in instructing the child, remedy its faults; must give him learning, and at the same time rear him to have a spiritual nature. Let the teacher be a doctor to the character of the child, thus will he heal the spiritual ailments of the children of men.[10]

Equating inactivity in children with dullness and slow-wittedness, and imagining that every intelligent child is inevitably clever and active is a supposition which is held by many people, but which is not upheld by experience and reality. Many children regarded as lazy or listless are very intelligent, show keen mental alertness, and are endowed with marvellous talents, while many who do not have the same intellectual capacities and are bereft of talents are none the less industrious, hard-working, and highly active.

Laziness and sluggishness cannot, therefore, be attributed to lack of intelligence, but rather to other causes which must be thoroughly investigated and understood before steps can be taken to improve the child's attitude.

Perhaps readers in their everyday lives have dealt with children who exhibit above-average intelligence and aptitude within the school environment and who do exceptionally well in their studies, but who are lethargic and lazy when it comes to physical work, at which time they 'don't want to get their hands dirty'.

The writer is personally acquainted with some extremely clever and talented children who are very active and alert at school, but who yawn and lounge around at home, reading magazines and daydreaming. If they feel sleepy, someone else has to prepare their beds, and if they want water, somebody else has to stretch out his hand to get it. They carry out their daily chores as though they were crippled or afflicted with feeble nerves. They seem to have no energy; sometimes they even seem to be ill.

Brief descriptions of different types of inactivity in children and their causes, as well as a consideration of methods to overcome them, follow:

Children who perform sluggishly fall into one of three groups:

1. Children who, because of different physical infirmities, become sickly, incapacitated, lethargic, and gloomy, cannot do their school work well, and are not nimble in their movements.

2. Children who, because of brain abnormalities, are afflicted with serious mental disorders, and as a result do not have the capacity for intellectual work.

3. Children who are healthy and strong but behave sluggishly, and have little patience for doing certain tasks.

As to the first two groups, we cannot go into detail here because of the complicated and delicate nature of the subject, and the difficulties which arise in trying to make accurate diagnoses. Children in this condition should be taken to medical specialists, and sometimes to psychologists as well, to obtain their opinions and assistance. The important point is this: as soon as signs of lethargy, sluggishness, or what people commonly refer to as 'laziness' begin to show themselves, the parents must set about finding the remedy, and not leave such children to themselves. And, of course, they should not accuse the children of being lazy and self-indulgent.

Concerning the third group, however, it can be said that:

1. The causes of lethargy in these children often arise from the conflict between the task which is assigned to them and their inborn inclinations. For instance, a child who displays agility in sports like basketball and swimming, and is interested in such activities as arts and crafts, finds that he is bored stiff in class while studying mathematics or Latin roots – a clear indication that the teacher has been unable to stimulate the child's interest in these subjects. To overcome the child's boredom in these and related cases, the work should either be made interesting and pleasing to him, or it should not be assigned, because tasks which are diametrically opposed to children's way of thinking and mental capacities arouse in them feelings of aversion and fatigue.

2. Gifted and intelligent children who make use only of their mental capacities and do not engage in physical work of any sort are primarily interested in performing 'brain-related' work, and avoid contact with tasks requiring the use of the physical faculties. These children, for instance, can devote endless hours to solving mathematical problems, but a half-hour of gymnastics or callisthenics is out of the question. If boys, they avoid such chores as watering the garden, gathering wood, or shovelling snow; if girls, they flee from washing dishes, cooking, sewing, and the like.

It is indubitably clear that the bodies and mental

capacities of children should be trained and developed simultaneously. Both boys and girls should be encouraged to participate in sport, physical activities, and everyday tasks so that their bodies and minds develop together, and the two sides of the scale are brought into balance. The sluggishness and lethargy exhibited by these kinds of children will then disappear, and no opportunity will be left for parents to scold them for their 'laziness'.

5

PRACTICAL CONSIDERATIONS FOR PARENTS

... every malady afflicting the body of man is an impediment that preventeth the soul from manifesting its inherent might and power.[1]

Let them also study whatever will nurture the health of the body and its physical soundness, and how to guard their children from disease.[2]

EVERYONE HAS HEARD the saying 'a sound mind in a sound body'; even in ancient times the relationship between a sound mind and a healthy body was clearly recognized. Nevertheless, in our age, which is regarded as an era of knowledge and inventions, an era considered unique in spreading far and wide the light of education and for discovering the unknown – mothers and fathers pay scant attention to this topic; it is a rare thing to find a parent who is conscious of the relationship between the growth of children and their training and education. There can be no doubt that lack of attention to this point can cause irreparable damage to young children, and shatter the foundation of their future happiness.

A gardener looks forward to the day when his tender saplings will have become tall and sturdy, producing choice fruits for many years. He will, of course, attend to their growth and development, and protect them from harm. By the same token, if fathers and mothers expect their children to grow up resourceful and skilful, to possess penetrating thoughts and sound judgement and not lag behind their friends and peers, then they should use every means at their disposal to safeguard their children's health and assure their natural growth and development. It is not logical to expect noteworthy accomplishments from possessors of weak and weary bodies; a parent who does so can be likened to a person who stacks a heavy burden on a weak and scrawny horse and whips it to a gallop.

Undeniably, we must accord physical health and hygiene the utmost importance. For the body is an instrument of the soul; the soul itself being a divine trust whose power and perfections are manifest in this world through the physical body, and whose attributes are realized through the medium of bodily members and organs. When a weak body is the bearer of the soul, it is as if someone wishes to travel freely and swiftly and vie with others in reaching his destination, but is handicapped by a weak and feeble horse. Parents should do their utmost to safeguard the health and well-being of their children. To ignore this matter is to open the door to a variety of detrimental consequences which will cause great distress and regret. Picture the following situation:

A child wakes up at seven o'clock sharp. His one thought is to get ready quickly so as to be at school before the bell rings one hour later. Since it takes him several minutes to walk to school, he has barely forty minutes between the time he gets up and the time he must leave the house. The child is not accustomed to discipline and order, and since the parents usually do not supervise him at this time of the day, he cannot benefit fully from this brief interval and his preparations do not go smoothly at all. Some of his time is used up in the search for clothes – uniform, socks, shoes and the like – because the night before these items had not been put away, but lay scattered in all directions. When he slips into a shoe, he is sharply reminded that a small nail had poked its point up through the insole on the previous day and hurt his foot. A great uproar shakes the house from stem to stern; hammer, pestle, and different-sized stones appear from all sides and the irksome nail is flattened. This performance coincides with a radio announcement telling the child that he has no more time to spare! He darts into the bathroom, wets his hands, goes through the motions of splashing water on his face, and, without brushing his teeth, rushes back into the kitchen where he spies his mother. 'Hurry up and give me something to eat, Mum,' he says. 'In fifteen minutes the bell will ring. I'll have to leave without having breakfast.' So saying, he goes after his school bag.

The mother swiftly and sternly retorts, 'Get in here and put something in your mouth. At least you can sit down and have a piece of toast.'

The child struggles to hold back his tears and says, 'Can't you see that I'm late? It will be noon before I can eat anything.' After further verbal exchanges, the child puts a piece of bread in his mouth, half chews it, and swallows it with or without the assistance of milk or tea; clutching another piece of bread in his hand, he tears down the road that leads to school.

Soon after, hunger pangs begin to bother the child.

Throughout the morning he entreats his friends to part with a portion of their snacks. One pupil offers him some peanuts, another one gives raisins; a candy bar and some potato chips come from two other sympathetic friends. This combination of food creates havoc in his stomach, and when he returns home his pale cheeks and bent posture immediately tell the mother that he has a severe stomach-ache. A lengthy discussion about medicine and treatment ensues, and lunch is completely forgotten. Even if the child had returned home 'happy and healthy', the mixture of food sticking to the walls of his stomach would hardly admit of an appetite.

Or let us suppose that he has worked up an appetite for food before returning home. Because discipline is in short supply during the midday break, hygiene is neglected at this time too. From the moment the child returns home, he has a little over an hour in which to eat, rest, and be back at school. As soon as he opens the door, his first words are, 'Is lunch ready, Mum?' The mother, who is busy preparing beans, or grating onions for the hamburger, or peeling carrots for the soup, or putting rice on to boil, replies in the negative, and adds: 'How did you get home so soon? Did you get out of school earlier than yesterday? Wait a while; lunch will be ready soon.' No matter how hard the child tries to convince the mother that he has come home at the usual time, she sticks to her guns and says, 'Anyway, the lunch is not ready.'

The child soon sees the futility of continuing the argument, and his thoughts turn towards a quicker remedy, which comes in the form of a peanut butter and jam sandwich; this, together with a little milk, tides him over until lunch time. But when the table is set and the child is called to eat, he no longer has the same appetite that he had when he returned home. He sits at the table and toys with his food, nibbling a little here and there; soon he directs his steps back to school, without the benefit of a rest. At supper, more unpleasant moments await the child. And so it goes on.

Of course, many people are careful and concerned about the health of their children, and their attention prevents many unfortunate occurrences. If, for instance, the mother gets up early enough, she can prepare breakfast and call the children at the proper time. She can supervise all their affairs with such words as 'Wash your hands and face well, darling; comb your hair nicely, and brush your teeth. Chew your food well, but don't waste your time – you have to leave soon . . .'

Every night, the mother should see that each child puts his books and clothes where they belong so that there is no need to search for them in the morning. She should also make sure that he does not stay up late in the evening without reason, that he has ample time for breakfast, and that lunch is ready on time so that his appetite is not ruined by eating snacks.

This care and attention needs no special knowledge, entails no extra expenditure, and will prove to be most effective in maintaining the health and well-being of the child while eliminating many potential hazards.

Height and Weight

The height and weight of a child and the relationship they have to his psychology are subjects which competent authorities have thoroughly researched. A characteristic sign of a child's state of health is normal growth in height coupled with regular increases in weight; parents ought to be concerned if the height and weight of their child are not within the range regarded as normal for his age.

In order to set their minds at ease, many mothers, when they see that their child is thin and weak, take this view: 'The reason my child looks thin is because he is growing so quickly. He was very chubby when he was younger; probably he will soon put on some weight again.' These mothers should be reminded that an increase in a child's height should be accompanied by a proportional increase in his weight. If a child's weight does not keep pace with his height, the cause should be discovered and remedied by competent specialists. One of the characteristics of childhood is the rapidity of bodily growth and development, and experts in this field have recommended that parents take care to safeguard the balance between height and weight during these 'growing years', particularly between the ages of three and eight, and not let their children become weak and underweight. The greatest influences on the growth of children, apart from heredity, are climate, nutrition, environment, and, more especially, sunlight.

Children from different countries do vary: a height that is tall for one country may be normal for another. The important thing is the relationship between height and weight. The following chart shows some typical statistics for three different countries. The samples included boys and girls between the ages of three and eight.

AGE	COUNTRY A				COUNTRY B				COUNTRY C			
	Height		Weight		Height		Weight		Height		Weight	
	Girl	Boy	Girl	Boy	Girl	Boy	Girl	Boy	Girl	Boy	Girl	Boy
3	89·7	93·2	13·0	14·5	85·4	86·4	12·4	12·5	92·0	93·0	14·0	14·0
4	96·8	95·0	15·3	15·7	91·5	92·7	13·9	14·0	98·0	99·0	16·0	16·0
5	99·5	103·0	16·4	16·5	97·4	98·7	15·3	15·9	103·0	104·0	17·5	17·5
6	106·7	106·6	18·2	18·2	103·1	104·6	16·7	17·8	107·0	109·0	19·0	19·0
7	110·2	111·2	19·2	20·2	108·7	110·4	17·8	19·7	113·0	115·0	22·0	22·0
8	113·2	113·8	21·0	21·0	114·2	116·2	19·0	21·6	118·0	120·0	24·0	24·0

Height is shown in centimetres, weight in kilograms

Safeguarding Children's Eyesight

The eyes, the most cherished parts of the human body, are virtually indispensable in the acquisition of knowledge. If their functioning becomes impaired during childhood through lack of proper care or hygiene, the innocent children will suffer inconvenience and hardship until the end of their lives; the acquisition of knowledge and the development of their perceptive powers will be much harder for them. The sense of sight is therefore like a precious jewel which should be protected at all costs. But regrettably, eye abnormalities rank amongst the most common disorders occurring during childhood. Careful studies have shown that new-born babies are far-sighted; little by little their eyesight becomes normal.

As this book is for parents, and not for schools, some of the following points may be relevant only at home.

1. Children should not read and write without an adequate lighting system, and should especially avoid studying by natural light at sunset.

2. While studying, the source of light should be overhead and to the left.

3. The distance between the eyes and the pages of a book with normal-size type should be in the range of 30 to 35 centimetres.

4. Chair and desk size should correspond to the height of the child, assuming proper posture.

5. Writing and reading on the floor is not good for the eyes because it causes the child to hunch over his books; this applies to reading while lying down as well.

6. One should never read while walking or moving.

7. If a child has to hold reading material closer to the eyes than is recommended, and if he does not see clearly things placed at a distance, he should have an eye test arranged.

Burdening Children's Memories

The influence which the faculty of memory exerts on our mental activity throughout our entire lives is unquestionably clear. This God-given bounty manages and directs all affairs pertaining to the mind: if the mind did not possess the ability to retain thoughts, then our mental activity would be fruitless, our connection with past events severed, and the scope of our knowledge limited to the here and the now.

The writer's purpose is not to delve into scientific descriptions of the memory, since this is a major subject in the study of psychology and besides, a later chapter deals with the memory and how to strengthen it. The objective, rather, is to point out to parents the harm which can result from overtaxing a child's memory.

Every healthy child is naturally endowed with a sound memory, but it must be understood that this power – not unlike many other capacities and characteristics – can be strong, average, or weak in different people. If the educators of the child are familiar with the best way to treat this inner power, and if they observe moderation in its use, the child will benefit; if, on the contrary, their approach is unskilful and puerile, immeasurable harm to the child will result. Man may be regarded as 'a mine rich in gems', including the memory; to make the best use of this wealth he needs intelligence, mental alertness, and – above all – practice.

The memory is normally very strong throughout the childhood years: whatever the child sees or hears is recorded, often as a result of repetition, which is more important than anything else for mental retention. Educators, however, are inclined to exploit this divine gift, and many mothers and fathers, for different reasons, add their load to the work horse, seemingly unaware that the hour will come when the horse will fall to its knees, and the rider, only part of the way along his journey, will find himself in a desperate situation. It is therefore essential that educators pay attention to certain points:

1. A memory can be either good or bad. Those who do not possess a good memory are unable to grasp, retain, and associate matters easily, nor can they learn or recollect a subject as readily as can those who have a good memory. It is not reasonable, therefore, to have

the same expectations of two children when one possesses a weak memory and the other a strong one; they cannot be treated alike. Lack of attention to this principle has led many parents to belittle and embarrass their children in front of their peers.

2. Weak and unhealthy children who have defects in their nervous systems, or who suffer from digestive disorders or irregular gland secretions, generally do not have good memories. Instead of putting pressure on such children to memorize lessons and master the various academic courses so as not to lag behind their friends and classmates, parents should seek the remedies to their illnesses, and try to cure their children of these physical disabilities patiently and compassionately, for by removing the cause, the effect will also be eliminated.

3. Regardless of which type of memory children have, good or bad, to burden this faculty is harmful. Children should not be forced to memorize poems or to learn incomprehensible things. Memorizing poems and prose can be beneficial if they are made use of in everyday life, or if they are essential for strengthening the memory. Otherwise, committing things to memory which are unnecessary, which can never be put to practical use and hence will be eventually forgotten, can only produce trouble. In short, it is evident that we must cling to moderation in this case too.

Fatigue

The effect of fatigue on children has long been a focal point of research: psychologists and child psychologists, with the assistance of physiologists, have conducted extensive studies into it. Here is a summary of the most important points:

1. Exhaustion is of two kinds: *(a)* superficial and temporary fatigue which dissipates with a little rest, restoring the consumed energy; *(b)* deep and prolonged fatigue which causes mental and physical exhaustion, requiring not only rest and relaxation in order to recuperate, but more effective measures such as a long period of recreation, a change of climate, and medical treatment.

2. The causes of fatigue are not the same for everyone. That is to say, people are not equally affected by, and do not tire the same amount from, similar physical and mental activities. But the structure of the body, the mental condition, and personal habits have a great influence on the degree of exhaustion which is felt. If a person gets used to a task and enjoys it, and surmounts all unpleasant obstacles through his determination to attain a goal, then of course he feels fatigue much later than a person who lacks these traits.

3. By 'exhaustion' is meant that a person is afflicted with a condition whereby he cannot replenish his energy by any other means except through sleep and rest. Certain types of physical and mental fatigue do not affect everyone, and can be cleared up by other means as well. People experiencing hysteria, for instance, feel weary without working or expending energy, and this type of tiredness subsides through the power of suggestion and reasoning.

4. In the opinion of physiologists, real exhaustion consists in this: a deficiency of essential bodily el-

ements, and the production of poisons in the body when performing work.

5. When physical tasks are performed, the organs of the body (even the brain, which is the central point of the nervous system) become fatigued; mental work tires the body as well. As a consequence, one cannot say that gymnastics, fencing, swimming, mountain-climbing, and similar sports, are forms of relaxation following mental work. Such sports intensify bodily exhaustion produced at the time of mental work. Nothing but complete rest and deep sleep will take away this exhaustion. Even if we engage in no special work during the day, come nightfall, it is certain that we need rest and sleep. Ernst Meumann, the nine-teenth-century German scholar who was a pioneer in experimental pedagogy, believed that gymnastics and physical exercises tire and exhaust the brain of a child just as much as mental work; also, more recent re-search has shown that exhaustion caused by solving mathematical problems is comparable to that caused by physical exercise.

6. Young children tire quickly both physically and mentally. One distinguishing sign of their fatigue is insomnia, which is children's dangerous enemy, for it deprives them of rest and prevents them from replen-ishing their energy.

7. Severe fatigue in children produces many and complicated effects. The following are among them: the attention span shortens; comprehension weakens; memory nearly stops functioning; absent-mindedness occurs; the rapidity and sharpness of the thinking process diminish; the state of happiness, cheerfulness, and joy, turns into sadness, gloominess, and distress;

overtired children do not study nearly as well as other children; their muscles diminish in strength and their body movements become uncoordinated; they often make mistakes when reading and writing; they do not react normally to external factors; their thoughts are not very deep or intense; their creative abilities diminish. A tired child is very nervous, irritable, and easily provoked, and is always angry; in class, he is not able to think clearly; his mind and brain are highly irritable, and this causes insomnia; he has no patience for work requiring concentration, nor for order and discipline in his affairs, and he is careless in everything; often he is pale, and his blood circulation is not normal; he over-reacts to natural occurrences and environmental changes; his body has little resistance to neuroses, weaknesses in the nervous system, and related conditions, and is always susceptible to different diseases.

Scientific principles have been established for evaluating the level of physical and mental exhaustion in children. As a result, scholars have been able to make suggestions to school teachers concerning the preparation of programmes, methods of teaching, and how to make the best use of a child's time. Further discussion of this matter is off the subject of our presentation, but it is necessary to mention some points to the parents, and especially the mothers. These deal with family life, and are concerned with preventing exhaustion in children. By observing the following recommendations – which are given by experts – as far as they are able, parents can protect their children from a great danger.

1. When children come home for lunch and have to return to school right away, they are tired. Mental work and physical activity (from morning until noon) have weakened the children's mental and physical faculties. Therefore they should refrain from playing, exercising, and doing homework during this short interval. Also, they should either have a nap or lie down quietly without moving for a few minutes so that the body can refresh itself as much as possible from the half-day of work, and ready itself for the remainder of the day. If time permits, they should also spend several minutes out in the open air, but without running about or other physical activity.

2. When children return home in the afternoon, in all probability they are worn out. They should not start studying immediately, nor should they engage in intense physical activity. If there is housework to do they may help with that first, and then, if possible, spend some time out in the open air for relaxation before getting involved with their homework.

3. Taking breaks from study at regular intervals very effectively reduces fatigue. When students are doing their homework, they should keep this in mind, and should take a fifteen-minute break after every thirty or forty-five minutes of work.

4. The best method for everyone (and especially children) to renew their supply of energy, is through deep and regular sleep. Nothing except sleep reduces exhaustion. The parents, and particularly the mothers, should derive as much benefit as they can from this God-given opportunity for rest and never reduce the sleep of their children. They should avoid taking chil-

dren out with them in the evening, a practice which is common in all strata of society. Not only can this have harmful moral effects – a topic which requires a separate discussion – but it also harms the health of the children.

Innumerable studies have dealt with sleep and its invigorating effect on children. Mothers are recommended that:

1. They should get young children in the habit of sleeping sometimes on their right sides and sometimes on their backs so that the functioning of the heart is not interfered with and no undue pressure is exerted on other parts of the body.

2. They should not serve children a heavy meal before putting them to bed, for food which is not easily digested disturbs children's sleep.

3. Excessive use of liquids such as coffee, strong tea, or other stimulants, which in general are harmful for the health of children, should be avoided.

4. They should take care to clean and ventilate the children's rooms and beds every day, and they should air out their mattresses and expose them to sunlight frequently. Insects in the children's bedrooms should be got rid of through hygiene.

The following table gives a general indication of how much sleep children ought to have.

Age	Number of hours out of 24
Suckling babies:	16
up to 4:	13
4–7:	12
8–12:	10
12–15:	8–9

In general, healthy children can get by with less sleep than can children who are weak or exhibit nervous tendencies. But if parents were to put into practice these counsels which have been carefully researched by specialists, a significant decrease in the number of nervous children would result.

Avoid Evening Visits with Children

The practice of going out for evening visits and passing time in one another's homes is a custom which is prevalent among all strata of society. If it were limited to grown-ups, and if children did not go to such gatherings, then the matter would not be worth mentioning in articles dealing with education. But since parents usually take their children along when they go visiting, a few comments about the harmful effects of this practice on the education of children are necessary.

1. Children, especially those who must get up early for school, should be in bed early. They need at least eight hours of undisturbed sleep so that they do not feel tired and lethargic when they wake up. Staying up late at night has a disastrous effect on children's sleep. If they miss part of a night's sleep, they will wake up feeling sluggish, not having replenished all their energy, and, in addition, they will not be able to concentrate on their lessons at school. As this sleep pattern continues, the children become increasingly weak and feeble.

2. During these visits, a considerable number of

people often congregate in a single room, and the air may become contaminated with cigarette smoke. The poor children, after sitting in school from morning until sunset, must now spend several hours in a stuffy room, where they get headaches, their bodies absorb poisons, and their nerves become irritable. At night, they will not be able to sleep peacefully, and will wake up feeling tired and nervous, with the daily routine in the same schoolrooms awaiting them. Such circumstances will eventually rob the children of their health. Pale complexions, nervous exhaustion, and digestive disorders all stem from this incorrect and unwise action.

3. The type of entertainment which takes place at these evening gatherings runs counter to a child's well-being. For children, whether they have eaten their supper or not, will, if they are not wisely supervised, consume excessive amounts of whatever is being served – nuts, biscuits, cakes, sweets, and so on – thereby putting an added burden on their stomachs. It is self-evident that the physical and mental faculties are impaired when digestive irregularities occur.

4. At these evening gatherings, grown-ups have a tendency to tell stories dealing with aspects of their daily lives which include personal and private matters, and they engage in these discussions unhampered by any consideration for the children in their presence. If someone who is even slightly familiar with the psychological make-up of children is present at the gathering, he will be dismayed at the extent to which the uninformed parents are careless in educational matters, as, with their own hands, they lay the groundwork for the

deviation of their loved ones from the path of virtue. If spicy jokes are added to these conversations, it will be seen that they have the effect of an axe striking at the root of children's morals.

It is clear that children listen carefully to all the subjects under discussion, storing whatever they hear in their hearts and souls. In later years, these seeds sown in the fertile field of each child's being will germinate and grow, and, more often than not, yield bitter fruits.

Summer Holidays and Their Importance for Children

Fathers and mothers are well aware how greatly school children become exhausted and worn out during the academic year, inasmuch as they have no opportunity whatever to rest. The school curriculum is designed in such a way that students must constantly draw on their store of physical and mental energies. Except for the hours of sleep, which are often uneasy and troubled because of exhaustion, they have no opportunity in which to replenish their energy supply.

The school student must rise early in the morning – at least by seven o'clock. Following his religious devotions, he gulps down his breakfast and has to be in school at eight o'clock, where he remains hour after hour in crowded, stuffy rooms, concentrating on learning his lessons. He then goes home and has lunch. Although the body is in need of rest after eating – the blood is directed towards the stomach to digest the food, causing signs of lethargy to appear in all parts of the body – the student nevertheless exerts himself, and, fighting off his natural and sound inclinations, returns to school and sits in those same crowded rooms whose air, in the winter season, is hardly ventilated. He then proceeds – to use an example – with the solving of mathematical problems, although mental exertion under these conditions may cause harm to the body. He returns from school around sunset. After all this, the exhausted child has to study and do his assignments for the next day. And then, completely fatigued and with weak nerves, he goes to sleep. From the fatigue, nervous exhaustion, and lack of fresh air during the day, it is clear that he will not be completely relaxed during the sleeping hours.

A school student works for nine months or more in this way, depleting his strength, and at the end of the academic year he is so completely debilitated that even the colour of his face indicates the extent of his physical and mental exhaustion, causing the parents real concern. The detrimental effects of this schedule are manifested to a greater degree in younger children; these tender plants of the divine garden do not have the strength to endure such long hardship, and so they become run-down more quickly, and are often afflicted with different diseases which are caused by their lack of bodily strength.

The summer vacation clearly offers an unequalled opportunity to replenish the mental and physical resources of children, and parents should make full use of it. If fathers and mothers choose to observe the following points, the summer season will prove to be highly beneficial to their children.

1. If at all possible, parents should take their children away from the city so that they are able to spend

their time in the fresh air and natural surroundings of the countryside; at night, they can brighten their eyes with the luminous moon and stars, and they can spend their days under the shade of trees, beside waterfalls, or at the foot of a mountain, and set in motion their listless and unused bodies – which have become like rusted machines. It is the time for children to swim, run and go mountain-climbing, and compensate for the months of stagnation and torpidity.

2. If parents are obliged to stay in the city, and are unable to take their children to the country, they should refrain from burdening them with physical and mental work. For instance, parents should not enrol their children in extra summer courses, nor engage them in physical tasks such as working as an errand boy or apprentice in shops or businesses: they should counsel them against wearisome and exhausting work. If a child, out of interest and of his own accord, busies himself with reading a beneficial book, so much the better, but parents should not through force and coercion oblige them to read books on difficult subjects which require thinking and concentration.

3. The most suitable method for revitalizing the body is deep and peaceful sleep. Young children need at least eight or nine hours of sleep, and since they have ample free time in summer, this sleep should never be sacrificed. Mothers (and sometimes fathers, as well) have a tendency to reason that children can go to bed late at night and get up late in the morning because they do not attend school in the summer and do not have anything to do. The fact is that going to sleep long after midnight is like staying awake, for when children alter their proper sleeping hours they will not

derive sufficient benefit from their nightly rest. Besides this, when adults get up early in the morning and prepare to go to work or do the housework, the quietness and tranquillity which are basic to deep and peaceful sleep will be disturbed. How then can the children continue sleeping? This kind of sleep will only result in sluggishness and feebleness.

The summer season, in short, should be considered a resting season for school children.

Nervous Children

A significant number of mothers and fathers share the opinion that nervousness in children is an inherited trait, passed down from parent to child. Although this attitude does have some basis, it is nevertheless incorrect to make generalizations in this case. It often happens that parents with a nervous condition bring healthy and calm offspring into the world; later on those healthy and relaxed children gradually become nervous and quick-tempered because of a lack of sound educational practices, disturbances in the home, and detrimental acts on the part of relatives and grown-ups.

In general, a nervous child is highly sensitive and very little provocation is needed to upset him. His sleep is far from peaceful: he may wake up several times in the course of a night, sometimes screaming and crying as though he were afraid of something, and making it very difficult to quieten him. When he is playing with friends he frequently becomes cross, and cries for the slightest reason; if his feelings get hurt, he breaks up the game. He is compulsively hyperactive: his hands, feet, and even his tongue seem to be constantly in motion. No sooner does he finish one thing than he starts doing something else. But he tires easily, and at times is so overcome with sluggishness that he has little patience for anything.

It is not unusual for nervous children to be talented, clever, and capable of learning skills quickly. But they tend to misdirect these abilities, and more often than not waste their energy, tiring and weakening themselves by excessive movement and exertion.

What are the causes of this type of behaviour? It is clear that most nervous children were not born that way, but acquired this characteristic during later stages of life. That is, nervous disorders are not innate, in most cases, but are brought about by external factors. If the family environment is constantly in a state of confusion, if the conduct of the grown-ups – especially the relationship between the parents – is not based on love and affection, and if arguments and differences regularly occur between the father and the mother, then the nerves of the children early on become wearied, exhausted, and impaired, and the children themselves develop into sickly and feeble individuals.

The nerves of children are like strings coated with gunpowder, and the damaging behaviour of parents like a match which, striking the string, ignites it immediately. Children absorb everything they see and hear as a sponge absorbs water, and it is for this reason that estrangement and coarse behaviour in the family damage children's nerves. If, while fathers and mothers are engaged in a heated argument, they chance to glance at their hapless offspring, they will notice how pale and listless they are. From the muscular spasms on their children's faces and their trembling lips, the parents will realize the extent of the children's inner turmoil caused by the tumultuous storm around them. The full weight of this suffering and torment is centred on the nerves, and only on the nerves.

Some suggestions for preventing and rectifying nervous disorders in children are as follows:

1. Under no conditions whatsoever should young children witness any of the unpleasant incidents which may occur between parents, or among friends and relatives.

2. Sharing the same bedroom with children can harm their health. Whenever possible, children should sleep in a room separate from their parents. The wisdom of this is clear to everyone, and is not in need of explanation.

3. Even though we have compared children to sponges, describing how they absorb whatever they hear and see, the analogy breaks down at a certain point, for a child, in his attempts to imitate grown-ups, exerts the utmost effort to repeat and mimic anything he has heard or seen. When the people with whom he comes in contact are upset or angered by the slightest matter, the child – even though he was healthy and strong at birth and his nervous system without defect – often pretends to work himself into a rage, emulating his parents' behaviour. Little by little he becomes so practiced that it becomes second nature to him.

To prevent the establishment of this injurious affliction in young children, fathers and mothers, as well as other grown-ups, should keep careful watch over their words and deeds – at least when children are present – and should make every effort to control their own nervous outbursts. In this way, they will avoid setting bad examples for their loved ones.

4. Excessive strictness, endless instructions and injunctions, non-essential and inappropriate punishment, physical punishment, and the like, greatly intensify the state of nervousness in a child, and parents should never resort to their use. Striking and beating children are extremely blameworthy practices, and have detrimental consequences both physically and mentally. Physiologists believe that physical punishment, in addition to causing mental disorders, also impairs the nervous systems of children – further reason for parents to totally shun its use.

5. Some parents do not deal moderately with their children. That is, in the face of some forms of misbehaviour they let loose the full force of their harshness, and resort to the use of extreme strictness; at other times they react with warmth and affection. One moment, the screams and shouts of the mother and father as they punish their child can be heard all up and down the block, but several minutes later, this is supplanted by parental affection, and the hugs and kisses for that same mistreated child are in such abundance that the anger and wrath seem to have been unreal. This approach leaves the child worried, perplexed and uneasy, for he never knows how his parents will react to his behaviour – whether he will become the recipient of their love and affection, or the object of their wrath. It is evident, therefore, that parents should carefully examine the course of action which they themselves follow, and assure that it is based on sound

educational principles, and that it is clear-cut and well-defined.

6. Children who are born with weak nerves are able to recuperate gradually if they live in quiet family surroundings. It is important to consult competent doctors about their condition, and provide the means for their comfort and tranquillity.

7. The importance of adequate sleep for children cannot be over-emphasized. Youngsters who have nervous conditions consume more energy in everyday activities than do others their age, and the best way to replenish this energy is through relaxed and undisturbed sleep. The younger the child is, the more sleep he needs. In addition to their regular sleep, children need a day-time nap as well until the age of five or six, and this should generally last from one and a half to two hours. Even after this age, nervous children still need an afternoon rest of up to one hour. If they are unable to fall asleep at this time, it does not matter too much, since just lying down and relaxing help quieten the nerves to some extent. All children should go to sleep at fixed hours in the evening, and nervous children should not be permitted to sit up late at night for any reason.

Heredity

Heredity, and the effect it has on an individual's training, has always been an involved and abstruse problem from the scientific point of view. This is attested by the number of books published about it, and the varying and sometimes conflicting views of scholars. In our brief presentation it is not possible to describe the theories of such prominent thinkers as Charles Darwin, Hugo DeVries, Herbert Spencer, Hans Fisher, and others, nor are we able to explore the laws and rules comprising Mendel's theory of heredity. It is, however, essential that we mention a few points (whose influences are obvious in training and education, and which to varying degrees have found acceptance with all who are associated with this science) so that parents, by acquainting themselves with the effects which heredity has on training, can more fully recognize the seriousness of their responsibilities towards their children, and not disregard this indispensable matter.

1. Physical and mental disorders of the parents (even heart disabilities and similar afflictions) as well as any severe nervous convulsions which the mother experiences during pregnancy may have harmful effects on the foetus.

2. When anger, wrath, fear, and panic prevail, the composition of the blood changes significantly. From this, it is understandable that a calm and untroubled life for an expectant mother (which is conducive to joy, happiness, and tranquillity of mind) will have a positive effect on the development of the foetus's physical and mental faculties, for at this stage the mother's blood carries its only source of nourishment. Research has favoured the view that the quality of the food eaten by the mother, and the kind of recreation she takes, also influence the foetus.

3. Toxic diseases and the addiction of the mother to alcohol will undoubtedly have a pernicious effect on children. In the offspring of parents with such afflic-

tions, intelligence may be impaired, and they may be susceptible to committing crimes. Also, they may have mental disorders and nervous diseases.

4. Intermarriage between close relatives often produces offspring who are deficient both physically and mentally.

5. The predominant characteristics of a parent are usually transferred to the offspring; these, however, do not reveal themselves immediately, but gradually and at different stages of life, especially during puberty and adulthood. Mental and physical disorders sometimes remain in a state of latency during childhood and then manifest themselves at this later stage.

6. Even though children do not inherit exactly the same talents and intelligence as their parents, they are not devoid of their general effect. A child of a famous scientist and inventor, for instance, might become a good writer, a statesman, or a competent businessman.

Since both the good and bad qualities, the deficiencies and perfections, of parents have such a great influence on the training of children, both mothers and fathers should under all conditions be careful of their own conduct and behaviour; they should have no doubt that, if they so wish, they can either uplift their children towards happiness and felicity, or degrade and afflict them with misery. Towards this end, and ever mindful of their stupendous responsibilities, parents ought to observe this point conscientiously: their good or bad conduct affects not only themselves, but it also has a direct influence on future generations and on society, for the effect is successively transmitted from parent to offspring.

Rousseau introduces his priceless book *Émile* with the statement that God has created everything good, but in the hand of man, it has been transformed into evil. These words are undeniably true, for man has been created good, and the ability to reason, which distinguishes good from bad, has been established in him. His sight has been illumined with the light of guidance so that he may distinctly perceive the correct path from the path of error, and differentiate between good and evil, so that if he maintains his natural temperament, if he does not ignore the guidance of true educators, and if his God-given common sense is not destroyed, he will shun all defilement, perverseness, and falsehood. But if he ignores these bounties and deviates from the path of good conduct and praiseworthy character, which distinguish man from the animal, and if he turns towards sensual pleasures, he will surely destroy the foundation of his own happiness along with that of his offspring, and demolish their self-respect. He will bring into being children for whose training and education even the most skilful educators will find themselves inadequate.

We cannot, of course, go back in time, and are not able to correct what our ancestors have done. But we can find a solution for our present and future state, and free the coming generation of physical and spiritual impediments. We should heed the counsels and experience of eminent researchers and pay attention to certain points which are the result of studies carried out in all parts of the world.

1. Our young men and women who have reached the age of maturity and have the ability to understand

these subjects are aware that they are the fathers, mothers, and educators of the next generation. They should, therefore, observe moderation in all that pertains to their physical and mental faculties, as befits progressive, civilized, and creative human beings. They should not stray from the path of virtue and rectitude of conduct, neither should they resort to acts which will be detrimental to themselves and their future children. They should, in all their actions – in eating, in recreation, in entertainment – be vigilant, and always keep in mind that they are supposed to bring forth healthy children with sound minds and vigorous bodies, and that any deviation from the scientific standard of praiseworthy conduct in their lives will undoubtedly have a profound effect on their children.

2. When young men and women get married, they should know that the primary purpose of marriage is that children be forthcoming. They should, therefore, fully prepare themselves for the fulfilment of the sacred duty of parenthood. They should strengthen their minds and bodies for this purpose, organizing their lives in such a way as to accomplish this goal with greater facility. Since they are awaiting a precious guest whose arrival is so cherished, they should welcome him and serve him with all the means available to them, and protect him from every conceivable physical and mental misfortune.

3. Husbands should watch over and take complete care of their expectant wives, providing them with the means of comfort and relaxation in accordance with the guidance given by competent medical authorities. They should avoid any act which could provoke over-

excitement or cause a nervous condition, and they should pay attention to the adequacy of the nourishment of their wives, while not neglecting to refer them to doctors whenever necessary.

In other words, husbands should do everything within their power to assure that the foetus in the mother's womb may grow naturally and be protected from the very harmful effects of nervous disorders, so that when fully developed and brought into the world, it will not be weak and sickly, and can avoid being afflicted with pain and suffering until the end of its life.

4. Both parents should make every effort to avoid alcohol, smoking, and contagious diseases, because these are harmful to themselves and detrimental to their children.

5. Marriage between blood-relations should, as far as possible, be avoided, so that strong, vigorous, and capable children can be raised, more ready for the acquisition of human perfections.

If these counsels and guide-lines are diligently observed by parents, the tasks of instructors and teachers will prove to be much easier, and the children, in a brief span of time, will be ornamented with the beauty of praiseworthy manners and exemplary conduct.

As the poet Sa'dí says:

What a wonderful effect craftsmanship will have
upon a virgin gem;
but no amount of polishing will bring forth a gleam
in the dark iron.

6

CHILDREN AND FREEDOM

*Know ye that the embodiment of liberty and its symbol is
the animal. That which beseemeth man is submission
unto such restraints as will protect him from his own
ignorance and guard him against the harm of the
mischief-maker . . . True liberty consisteth in man's
submission unto My commandments, little as ye know
it.*[1]

*. . . a high standard of moral conduct is not to be
associated or confused with any form of asceticism, or of
excessive and bigoted puritanism. The standard inculcated by Bahá'u'lláh, seeks, under no circumstances, to
deny any one the legitimate right and privilege to derive
the fullest advantage and benefit from the manifold joys,
beauties, and pleasures with which the world has been so
plentifully enriched by an All-Loving Creator.*[2]

ONE OF THE great calamities that afflicts humanity in
our time is the unbridled rush towards excessive
liberty. The abandoning of old habits and customs is
accompanied by a general lack of attention to high
standards of moral conduct and spiritual truths, a
situation which has generated countless problems that
to some degree affect everyone. A considerable number of people take pride in being in the vanguard of
change and of giving the impression to others that they

themselves are totally free and unrestricted, shunning everything connected with the past.

If someone were to examine carefully the social relations of mankind as a whole, he would find abundant evidence in both the East and the West that moral standards have by and large been abandoned, and nothing definite has replaced them. In general, the code of behaviour observed by increasing numbers of people is marked by an excessive attachment to trivial and usually misdirected pleasures and to whatever offers instant gratification. And these excesses are clung to in the name of freedom!

Can anyone deny that gambling, excessive consumption of alcohol, sexual vices, drug addiction, irreligiousness, dishonouring of parents, and many similar things are wide-spread amongst the people of the earth, and that the arena of these transgressions is growing in such a way as to be a cause of great anxiety among the serious thinkers in society?

The writer has travelled through countries in all continents and has appraised, according to his own knowledge and understanding, the social conditions which exist in many different societies, and has personally witnessed the detrimental influence exerted by this strange 'liberty'. Following closely in the footsteps of grown-ups, pubescent children and adolescents give full reign to their sensual inclinations; in some cases, this age group has even surpassed others. It seems almost unbelievable that in many countries young students of both sexes have so come under the influence of sensuality that, at the beginning of their lives and by their own hands, their innate capacities and talents have been forfeited – yet it is so.

undue strictness, opposition to the
[uests of children, and preventing their
participation in healthy and legitimate recreation are
extremely harmful, but excessive freedom is so detrimental that its explanation is not an easy task. It is
essential to observe moderation, since both extremes
are blameworthy. Nothing necessary to children's
physical and mental growth and development should
be withheld from them, nor should they be left to do
whatever they wish, with no restrictions imposed on
the way they use their intellectual and physical powers.

If, because of the running and jumping, the playing,
the laughter, the conversation and stories of their
children, the parents become angry and try by rough-
ness and coarse language to quieten them and prevent
them from acting normally, then they are making a
grave mistake. The hapless children in such families
are put under a maximum of nervous tension. They
dare not express themselves in the presence of their
parents; they always have heart palpitations; they are
excitable, pale, and have a drooping posture as a result
of the inner pressure brought on by fear of the anger
and shouting of their fathers and mothers. These
parents are going to extremes to curtail the freedom
of their children, and are causing them distress and
unhappiness.

And as to the fathers and mothers who have very
little to do with their children's affairs, who have
totally banned the use of 'do's' and 'don'ts', who do
not inquire of these inexperienced youngsters – so
greatly in need of guidance – where they have been,
what they are planning to do, why they arrived home
at a late hour, with whom they are going walking, why

they have acquired such and such a bad habit, why they have turned their backs on prayer, what prompted them to buy indecent books, or why they sit around in the daytime and then have to stay up late to finish their homework – such parents have taken the opposite extreme. The importance of following the dictates of moderation in observing this educational point cannot be over-emphasized.

Street Corners and Back Alleys

Wings that are besmirched with mire can never soar.[3]

One of the three factors influencing children's behaviour is that environment, outside the school and away from the family, where children willingly, reluctantly, or out of necessity spend part of their lives.

There is one area of this out-of-doors environment which always has a pernicious effect on children from the educational point of view, and is never suitable for their training: this is the area comprising the street corners and back alleys. Educators should never adopt a positive attitude – or even one of non-resistance – towards this environment; they should always warn their children of its extremely harmful effects.

The reasons for this are many. First, passers-by are not usually bound by educationally sound principles, and do not observe those important and necessary matters that so greatly affect the morals of youngsters. They may say things and give vent to ideas that are not suitable for children and will have a negative effect on them. Second, some street vendors may not give due attention to the essentials of propriety, and if their acts and words do not accord with acceptable standards of morality, this will be harmful to the character of the children. Third, shiftless or mischievous delinquents may do things that can greatly damage the children's morals and psyche. And fourth, the children may encounter some misdirected playmates of the same age, who may speak or act in such a way as to be a bad example to them.

Some scholars believe that all actions are based on the S-R (stimulus-response) formula: that is, human beings are affected by, and react to, any stimulus. These stimuli can produce either good or bad effects on people. As a straightforward example, you feel an inner joy and happiness, and your face lights up, whenever you enter a garden and see beautiful lilies and daffodils, and hear the melodious bird-song. But if you pass by a war-torn and fetid area, you shrink back in disgust, overcome by feelings of sadness and melancholy.

This formula is applicable to children too, and since they react to all stimuli, and are affected by every word and deed, the back-alleys and street corners constitute one of the negative elements in their training. The harmful aspects of these areas are so many that they cannot be adequately listed. It may be that the children, while en route to school or for other unavoidable reasons, have no alternative but to pass through such places. We are seriously mistaken, however, if we willingly decide to lead our precious and innocent children unnecessarily to this kind of area, and leave them free and without supervision.

It has often been observed that some mothers send their children outside in order to have them off their hands 'for a few minutes'. And even if the child is not willing to go, the mother encourages him, saying, 'Why don't you go out and play with the other children?' or 'You have left such a big place to come and sit in the corner of a room?' Other mothers, while not encouraging their children to go out alone, nevertheless leave them free to choose.

The harmful effects on children of passing their time running around on their own are too numerous to be spelled out here. However, we will summarize some of the main points:

1. In the back alleys, and in gatherings on street corners, children are exposed to negative and harmful influences which, from the point of view of training and education, are unsatisfactory.

2. They become playmates with others who have been deprived of the guidance of an educator, and whose morals and behaviour have not been corrected. By becoming friends with disreputable and mannerless children, they are affected by their words and actions. The great influence which friends and companions have is clear to everyone.

3. When children develop the habit of whiling away their time on street corners, and taste the 'pleasures' of a 'free' life, where there is nobody to order them about and supervise their actions and behaviour, little by little they will have nothing to do with their homes or even their schools, which (as they see it) are brim-full of difficulties, pressures, restrictions, 'do's' and 'don'ts'. Escaping from the guidance of their parents and educators will always be uppermost in their thoughts.

4. On the streets, their health can be greatly impaired.

In short, any time spent by a child out on the streets

and away from the guidance and vigilance of his educators and parents, be it for recreation or to pass the time, is very dangerous both to the body and to the psyche of the child. Parents (especially mothers) must not give their consent to it, and must never with their own hands lead children along this path, which is truly lethal from the educational point of view. Naturally mothers should not get upset or angered easily, but should be forbearing and patient, and remain unruffled, because without patience and forbearance a mother cannot cope with the sacred duty of caring for children.

The impatient mother who leaves the children to themselves can be likened to a ship's captain who abandons his post in the middle of the ocean, leaving the passengers to reckon with the danger.

To avoid having the child develop a resentment for the home environment, and think only about spending his time on the street, the mother should not prevent him from moving about and playing (to the extent that is natural and instinctive to him) – harmless actions which are often misnamed 'naughty'. Also, the mother should not offend her children with unjustifiable 'do's and 'don'ts', nor should she direct harsh language to them. And she should be aware that only a statue can remain motionless and quiet in a corner, for if a child (in whom God has breathed life and whose mental and physical faculties are developing) is apathetic and slow in movement, it is a sign that he is ill. As far as she is able, the mother should provide her children with suitable playthings for their amusement, and busy them in some way so that they do not become 'naughty'.

Choose Good Companions

The company of the ungodly increaseth sorrow, whilst fellowship with the righteous cleanseth the rust from off the heart.[4]

Companionship with wrong-doers vexes the soul, tires the body and gradually pulls man down from a lofty station to the lowest abyss – like the angel in Sa'dí's poem whose spiritual aspirations are changed into devilish desires through association with a demon:

If an angel keeps company with a devil
it will learn terror, betrayal and guile.

Fellowship with good people, on the other hand, illumines the heart, uplifts the soul, ennobles the character of man and protects the light in the lamp of his heart from the winds of idle fancy and desire. This is the reason the Manifestations of God have warned men so strongly against companionship with evil-doers, and commanded them to seek communion with the righteous.

The purpose underlying this introduction is to emphasize one educational point: the greatest cause of moral corruption among pubescent children and adolescents is their companionship with bad friends who gradually steer them off the straight path of virtuous conduct, distract them from school and study, and eventually lead them to such misfortune that one cannot help but shed tears of regret for their condition.

However much you, the parents, observe the essential aspects of training in the home and protect your children from wrongdoing, as soon as your youngsters seek fellowship with bad friends out on the streets or at school, your efforts will be nullified, and the day will come when you will see that whatever you have so patiently woven at home will have been unravelled by others. Your most important duty as fathers and mothers, therefore, is to be ever watchful as to whom your children associate with outside the family. Do not content yourselves with knowing that the children are under your supervision at home, but rather devote part of your time – even though it may require cutting out non-essential things in your daily round – to finding out about your children's friends; as soon as you notice that guidance is necessary, try to find a solution either by relying on your own experience, wisdom and parental intuition, or by consulting experts. Keep in mind the age of the children and the type of problem involved. Spare no effort, for one minute of negligence will produce trouble a thousand-fold.

Whenever suitable occasions arise, the children should be counselled, guided and made to understand the detrimental consequences which are the outcome of fellowship with the wrong kinds of friends. Also, the school authorities can be included in the discussion, or, if necessary, the troublesome companions can be sought out and asked to stop associating with your children.

In short, one must make use of any means at his disposal in dealing with this difficulty. Just as a physical disease attacks the human body, causing pain or even dragging the afflicted person towards death, so also may any of hundreds of spiritual diseases befall the human spirit, impelling the afflicted person towards spiritual death. When someone has a contagious disease such as a cold or tuberculosis, you never permit your children to go near him; how then is it possible for you to allow them to associate with people in whom the signs of moral decay are evident, jeopardizing the souls of your loved ones?

Alcohol

The drinking of wine is, according to the text of the Most Holy Book, forbidden; for it is the cause of chronic diseases, weakeneth the nerves, and consumeth the mind.[5]

Become ye intoxicated with the wine of the love of God, and not with that which deadeneth your minds, O ye that adore Him![6]

Educators and scholars throughout the world, both past and present, have devoted their time and attention to assessing the harm that results from the consumption of alcoholic drinks, and the particularly detrimental effect which alcohol has on the development of children. The following points summarize their conclusions:

1. Alcohol is a lethal poison for individuals and a nightmarish calamity for society. It not only threatens those addicted to it with ruin, but also torments their innocent children with endless hardship, and the promise of an uncertain future. The use of alcohol induces a poisoning effect in human beings which is referred to as 'drunkenness' among the general populace. This poison paralyses the nervous system, unbridling its control over speech and actions. Discernment and determination inevitably weaken; if the person gets drunk habitually, mental and nervous disorders then occur, among them dipsomania,

Korsakoff's syndrome, and polyneuritis. With continued drinking, a disease develops whereby hallucinations are experienced; the person affected imagines that he sees strange creatures and hears frightening voices. His senses are disturbed, his hands tremble, he speaks incoherently, and the strength of his heart will weaken. After spending three to five days in this state, he falls into a long deep sleep. After the crisis, inflammation of the lungs and kidneys, and heart palpitations, may remain with him until the end of his life.

2. The toxic effect of alcohol is so intense that in some European countries an annual average of six thousand people die prematurely from continuous use of it, leaving their unfortunate children without their care, and perhaps depriving them of all material and spiritual bounties.

3. When the bread-winner of a family is addicted to alcohol, part of his earnings goes to support his addiction. This inevitably curtails the children's proper nutrition and leaves an unsatisfactory effect on their growth.

4. In families where the parents are regularly inebriated, they disregard courtesy and any semblance of dignity while in an inebriated state, and will in all probability commit such actions and utter such words in the presence of their offspring that the children's sense of shame will be effaced. Repeated occurrences lead the children to regard ugly deeds and unpleasant words as something normal, since their eyes and ears become accustomed to them. If they adopt the habits of their parents, there is no doubt that they will become so morally corrupt that their names will be of absolutely no significance on the scroll of humanity.

5. Alcoholism causes the appearance of sickly and weak children, physically defective and mentally imperfect. Sixty-six children out of a hundred whose fathers or mothers are addicted to alcohol have short memory spans, are less intelligent than normal children, and find difficulty in studying. Fully 17% are defective in hearing and speech, and 17% have weak muscles. In general, alcoholics do not produce totally healthy children.

6. In families where a drunken parent causes an uproar or creates a disturbance, the children, so greatly in need of tranquillity and rest, will be deprived of sleep; their nerves will become weak from fear and commotion.

7. Children who regularly see their parents in a drunken state shun their homes and despise their parents, looking upon them with contempt. They grow to regard their families as the focal point of malevolence and depravity. In seeking companions they may come to associate with disreputable persons, and fall, at last, under the influence of the most corrupt and bestial elements of society.

8. The children of such parents are always ashamed and made to feel disgraced in the eyes of their peers. They also experience intense grief, sadness, and distress.

9 .The following figures compiled by specialists serve to underline the harmful effect which alcohol has on children:

GROUP A: *Children who have not consumed alcohol*
42% made rapid and considerable progress at school

49% were average at school
9% did badly at school

GROUP B: *Children who occasionally consumed alcohol*

34% did well at school
56% were average
10% did badly

GROUP C: *Children who consumed alcohol daily*

27% did well at school
56% were average
15% were unable to study at all

A comparison of these figures shows that even if a small amount of alcohol is consumed by children daily, their mental faculties become noticeably impaired, and as a result they will be undeservedly deprived of acquiring knowledge and perfections. If they never drink alcohol, 42% of the children will continue their studies successfully, but if only a little bit of this poison enters their bodies daily, the figure decreases to 27%.

10. Tests were carried out to evaluate the physical strength of 515 boys and 554 girls who consumed alcohol regularly. Only 65 boys and 87 girls managed to show good results. The remaining 450 boys and 467 girls registered deficiencies.

11. Some parents who have been given unsound information maintain that wine and beer strengthen their children. They go against their innocent children's natural inclinations and give them alcoholic drinks. As previously mentioned, alcohol is a form of

poison which, on entering the human body, reduces its defensive capacity against sickness, making it highly susceptible to diseases which affect the liver, kidneys, lungs, and heart. In children, who are by nature delicate, the nervous system in particular is adversely affected. Alcohol will also gradually destroy their God-given talents, and make them quick-tempered, rough, and weak-willed; more important, their minds become weakened to such an extent that they will often appear to be stupid.

Now that we have seen, from a moral, social, and economic point of view, to what degree alcohol is harmful, and what kind of threat it poses to our children's very existence – children who should assume the places of their mothers and fathers and render service to society – we should seriously try to blot out this dangerous habit. Parents who cherish their children as they do their own lives – bearing hardship and trouble for their comfort and well-being and unwilling to see any misfortune befall them – should avoid alcohol completely, both for the sake of the happiness and honour of society, and so that they may raise healthy, vigorous, intelligent children, who will stand out distinguished from others. Our promising young people are, of course, included in these considerations, and they too should determine to avoid this repugnant habit.

Cinema and Television

. . . a chaste and holy life, with its implications of modesty, purity, temperance, decency, and clean-mindedness, involves no less than the exercise of moder-

ation in all that pertains to dress, language, amusements, and all artistic and literary avocations. [7]

No invention since movable type and the printing press has rendered a greater service in spreading knowledge than film, and no means have been so effective in bringing to light information about the uninhabited and remote areas of the earth. There can be no doubt that the names of the Lumière brothers (two French chemists who, in the year 1895, registered this important invention) ought to be remembered with respect. Film may be regarded not only as one of the best means of entertainment, but also as one of the best methods of explaining historical events, scientific subjects or geography, or for depicting civil and social perspectives. In developed countries, educators make great use of television films, video and cinema, and have noted, when using film for educational purposes, that children watch them with great zeal and eagerness. Here are some statistics, compiled before the impact of television, that indicate the degree of attraction between children and 'the movies'.

In England, in the city of Liverpool, 13,000 school children went to the cinema daily, while in Scotland, in Edinburgh, every school child went on average twice weekly; in New York, 10,000 children went daily. In some cities in Germany, 75% of all children went to the cinema twenty times in the course of a year.

Since these statistics were compiled, television has in these countries become an accepted part of a child's life, and the amount of time spent in front of the screen has risen noticeably. The temptation for parents to use the television as baby-sitter is irresistible – and for the child, television can become almost an addiction. Not only is he attracted to it, but he feels he cannot afford to miss a programme that his friends will be watching.

On the one hand, cinema and television are beneficial in education. On the other hand, if children are left totally to themselves in their choice of films, they may easily overstep the bounds of moderation and watch films that are damaging instead of educational. Many scholars and other intelligent people have brought to parents' attention the necessity of protecting their children from the harmful effects of watching films of low moral standard. The following points summarize the findings of studies on children and the cinema, but many of the results are applicable to television as well.

1. Children often go to the cinema either alone or accompanied by a friend, the choice of film depending on their own judgement. If the parents exercise no control in such an arrangement, the children will pick films which are completely harmful to their spirit and morals – and they are in no way protected from the unpleasant effects of these films.

In a children's questionnaire on this subject, Dr Langenberg recorded the following results: 653 children went to the cinema alone, 256 went with friends, 190 with brothers, 14 with sisters, 12 with both parents, 10 with the father, 1 with the mother. That is, out of a random sample of 1136 children, only 23 watched films while accompanied by one or both parents.

2. Left on their own, children will spend hours at the cinema, often watching the same film twice or even

three times. Sitting for long periods of time in stu
surroundings will, of course, be damaging to th...
health. To clarify the matter, the following figures
show the uninterrupted lengths of time that the children of one typical classroom spent at the cinema: 3
spent 1 hour, 2 spent 1½ hours, 2 spent 2 hours, 6
spent 2½ hours, 4 spent 3 hours, 3 spent 3½ hours, 9
spent 4 hours, 2 spent 4½ hours, 7 spent 5½ hours, 3
spent 6 hours, 1 spent 7 hours, and 1 spent 8 hours. Out
of forty-three school children, selected at random, the
majority stayed at the cinema for over four hours!

3. More often than not, children prefer films about
detectives, spying, thieves, romance, murder, armed
robbery, and so on, while they are not highly motiv-
ated to watch moral and educational films. Dr
Sternbüber, who studied what happens when nobody
supervises the child's choice of film, leaving him to
exercise this natural preference for 'exciting' films,
came to the following conclusions:

a. This type of film induces superficiality; the child
does not accustom himself to the thoroughness and
depth of realistic events.

b. By coming under the strong influence of the behaviour and actions of others, his own power of
creativity weakens.

c. His rate of comprehension will diminish, and he will
become deficient in the powers of perception and logic.

d. Lying and secrecy predominate, and he gets into the
habit of nonsensical recreation.

c. By frequently seeing films that are immoral (in the
widest sense of the word), his moral sense becomes
weakened, and he is inclined to commit immoral
actions.

f. Little by little, he destroys his health, becoming afflicted with impaired vision, weak nerves, and various respiratory diseases.

Many researchers believe that immoral films are a public and social hazard because they depict corrupt and indecent actions as something normal. As a consequence, children and adolescents (who are still under the influence of animal instincts, and in whom the foundations of moral education have yet to be strengthened) often see the wrongdoers as the heroes of the story, because they are usually applauded by the audience for their daring escapades. As the 'hero's' actions awe and amaze the audience each time, the innocent children come to regard corruption in a good light, and nourish in their impressionable minds the hope of becoming like him. Clearly, such a misleading example will draw the children away from moral excellence and human virtues. Such films often steer adolescents towards theft, violence, deviation from chastity, and disobedience to the laws of government.

Plas, in his comprehensive work on children and cinematography, observed that children who have just entered the stage of maturity and whose sexual interest has begun to function may well become bogged down in the mire of moral corruption as a result of frequently viewing romantic or pornographic films which are contrary to the standards of morality; these films are produced for the sole purpose of making money by gratifying the animal inclinations of lustful and capricious people. Such films must therefore be regarded as lethal poison for adolescents.

It is for these reasons that standards have been laid

down as a guide for children's attendance at the cinema. Films have been produced especially for children, taking into account the requirements of different age groups. Parents are urged to observe the regulations which have been established by their governments, and to apply the same principles to the television programmes they allow their children to watch.

Since children ought not to be deprived of the benefits of seeing films – after all, a useful invention – parents ought to make sure that their offspring go to the cinema or watch television on suitable occasions, while at the same time protecting them from the hazards. To do this, it is essential to pay as much attention as possible to the following suggestions:

1. Before taking children to the cinema, obtain a reliable description of the scenes in the film. If possible, see the film yourself first, and then, if you are satisfied that no harm can result, try to accompany your children when they see it. In evaluating the film, the point should be kept in mind that parents' own tastes are not the standard, as a film which is harmless to you may, for the reasons already mentioned, be harmful to your children.

2. Observe moderation; don't assume that every free evening should be automatically reserved for watching television or going to the cinema. A stroll in the open air is more invigorating for children than sitting in stuffy buildings.

3. Do not take very young children to see films. They neither enjoy seeing them, nor understand anything about them. Just being in the theatre makes them

restless, since its only effects are to deprive them of
clean air and curtail their rest.

4. When buying the tickets and choosing where to
sit, take into account any abnormalities in the children's eyesight. This means that near-sighted children
should sit closer to the screen than far-sighted children, so that their eyes are not unduly strained.

5. As far as possible, avoid sending children unaccompanied to the cinema.

6. Do not allow your children to stay at the cinema
for too many hours at a stretch, watching the same film
two or three times in succession.

7. Make the most of those amusing films which are
not harmful to children, as well as scientific, historical,
and geographical films.

As for adolescents, who are quite capable of distinguishing between good and bad without being in
need of the 'do's' and 'don'ts' of others – they, of their
own accord and just as they shun narcotics and
alcohol – should determinedly and with complete
understanding avoid seeing disturbing films harmful
to their temperament, morals, and psychological well-
being. This important subject, if put into practice, will
have a beneficial influence on their future.

The Importance of Suitable Books for Children

*Take the utmost care to give them high ideals and goals,
so that once they come of age, they will cast their beams
like brilliant candles on the world, and will not be defiled
by lusts and passions in the way of animals, heedless and
unaware, but instead will set their hearts on achieving
everlasting honour and acquiring all the excellences of
humankind.*[8]

Rarely is sufficient attention paid to the quality of the reading matter which falls into the hands of our children. Children are usually left absolutely free to select any books and magazines they want: since the importance of this subject is seldom recognized, parents often do not trouble themselves with the supervision of their offspring in this matter. And so, because of the negligence of the parents on the one hand, and the influence of friends on the other, and also because of their curiosity and infantile inclinations, children read almost anything they can lay their hands on, without distinguishing between good and bad.

The detrimental consequences of such a freedom are, of course, clear to every discerning mother and father. In the opinion of the writer, just as parents are concerned with their children's diet, taking care lest they come down with indigestion from eating the wrong things, so they should concern themselves, and to an even greater degree, with the development of their children's mental faculties, mindful lest something harmful find its way into their possession and cause 'spiritual indigestion'. For if something toxic reaches the mind, its pernicious influence will be far greater than the effect which unsuitable foods have on the body.

Magazines and newspapers are regularly brought into all homes, and are read by all adult members of the household. Since they are left lying around, the pre-adolescent and adolescent children read them too. Unfortunately, much magazine fiction is romantic, where the hero or heroine of the story is a man or a woman in love by profession. Some writers misuse their art form, putting on the printed page matters that have the effect of stimulating the sexual instincts of young people. If the reading of such stories is allowed to proceed unchecked, the reader will gradually fall prey to many mental and nervous weaknesses.

I shall briefly describe some of the harmful effects which the reading of love stories has on adolescent and pubescent boys and girls, and then present several methods recommended by specialists, so that parents may prevent their children from reading such material.

1. In whiling away their time reading love stories, the maturing children are deprived of books worth reading, whether literary or scientific, or even school textbooks. These stories have been attractively prepared in a daydreamy style, and naturally adolescents take delight in them; as a result, much of that time which should be spent on acquiring knowledge and human perfections is wasted. These children are like the unwary traveller who tore his bag full of gold coins; drachmas and dinars fell to the ground, until he realised what was happening, when he found he had no gold left.

2. Stories of love and romance are for young people a means of escape from the real world, causing the birds of their souls to flutter continually above the horizon of fancy and imagination – like a person in a deep sleep dreaming sweet dreams which differ greatly from actual life. Such stories affect adolescents like the poisons of hemp juice and opium, which destroy the inner faculties of perception, and cause the afflicted person to roam about in an imaginary world far removed from reality. If adolescents continue to read such books and shut themselves away from the real

phenomena of life, devoting their energy to wandering in a world of fancy, they become paralysed members of society. An example will help to clarify this point:

A boy (or girl) in early adolescence takes a story book – nowadays dignified by the name of 'novel' – to school along with his textbooks. Instead of listening to what the teacher says, he slips the book (which he considers appealing) under the lip of the desk and furtively reads it, wandering – by the power of his imagination through the peculiar world of the story, and stupefying his mind with the narcotic substance which lies concealed in the phrases of the book. Returning home, he reclines on the bed and, with particular pleasure, continues reading the book instead of preparing his school assignments. He is so influenced by its enticing scenes that his opinions about the actual world become altered – like someone who sees everything in shades of green when wearing green-tinted glasses. If his mother asks him to do some chore, her interruption of his chain of 'sweet' imagination upsets him. He will either ignore the request, or carry it out angrily and nervously.

3. If the authors have not restrained their pens, adolescents who read their stories experience severe excitement of the nerves, and their sexual drives begin functioning before the appropriate time and in a way which is unnatural. As a result, they will become burdened with blameworthy habits, detrimental both to their bodies and to their minds.

If all the pernicious results of reading romantic stories in adolescence were mentioned, this presentation would become too long. For the sake of brevity no further points will be added; a summary of some methods of preventing the reading of such books follows.

1. Fathers and mothers should continually keep watch over the books their child reads. From the very beginning, parents should raise the child in such a way that he will of his own accord show his parents his books and consult them about what he ought to read. If an unsuitable book falls into the hands of the child, the parents should be frank and tell him that reading such a book is not good for him. They should educate the child so that he will consult them – especially the mother – and welcome their guidance in all matters, whether trivial or important, including his reading.

2. With the utmost kindness and compassion parents should make sure that the child understands that whenever he wants to borrow a book from the library, or buy magazines or books, he must first consult his mother and father and obtain their opinions, and if it is recognized that the book is beneficial, he may read it, but otherwise it should be put aside.

3. The parents themselves should observe the dictates of wisdom and not keep in their homes newspapers or magazines which contain inappropriate articles for children and adolescents (or at least, they should not keep them at the disposal of their youngsters). In this way the child will be prevented to some extent from reading such things.

4. When the time is ripe and the adolescent child is prepared to listen, the parents should bring this point to his attention: just as a heavy and unsuitable meal

disturbs the stomach, discomfort spreading to all parts of the body, the same is true of a bad book, which will exhaust the reader's brain, diminish his powers of perception, and weaken and enfeeble his nerves. The child should be counselled not to read any book without first evaluating it, and the best way to have it evaluated and to distinguish a good book from a harmful one is to discuss it beforehand with his parents, or with some other knowledgeable and sympathetic person.

I wish to re-emphasize the point that parents should assist their children in selecting books and magazines, and prevent them, through the use of kind words and wise counsel, from reading distasteful things conjured up by writers who have put on paper whatever has come into their minds for the sole purpose of attracting the attention of readers. As far as possible, parents should avoid bringing home reading material which is unsuitable for children; rather, they should place beneficial books and articles at their disposal.

In pharmaceutical dispensaries, you may have noticed that in one section there is a sign displaying a skull and crossbones, with the word 'Poison' written beneath in large letters. The pharmacist separates poisonous substances from the other items so that he does not give something toxic to a customer by mistake. Perhaps if similar precautions were taken with unsuitable books and magazines brought into the home, children would take note of the 'Poison' signs, and would keep away from these noxious substances.

7

FOSTERING THE DEVELOPMENT
OF CHILDREN

*Children must be most carefully watched over, pro-
tected and trained; in such consisteth true parenthood
and parental mercy.*[1]

THE WISE, the accomplished, the learned and the scholarly, from the time of Plato until the present day, all
uphold the view that the family has a great influence
on the psychological makeup of children; the family
bears the greatest responsibility for training their
mental faculties, fostering sound morals and balancing
the development of mind and body.

Books on this subject constantly remind parents
that, just as they labour with heart and soul for the
development of the child's physical faculties, always
hoping that he will be healthy and strong and protected from injuries inflicted by the outside world – so
they ought to resolve to educate the child's intellectual
faculties and strengthen his moral fibre. For if a person
be deprived of spiritual qualities, human perfections
and praiseworthy conduct, he cannot become a source
of good for mankind, even though he be reared in
comfort and affluence, physically healthy, and skilful
in all the sciences and arts. The famous Persian poet
Sa'dí put the same thought in this way:

Generosity and kindness:
the true station of humanity,
and not this gruesome monster we appear.
Bereft of these qualities,
is there any difference between man
and a lifeless picture on the wall?

To depict the pervasiveness of the effect which the family exerts on the psychological make-up of our children, we will look at the results of the observations of Paul Bert, a world-renowned specialist. In his view, the following causes have a negative influence on the mental development of children and on their future; also, they will deprive the children of proper training and have other irreversible results:

1. The death of the father and/or mother.
2. Divorce and disunity in families.
3. Repeated trips by the father, and the children's periodical deprivation of his care.
4. Prolonged absences of the mother, and leaving the children with different people.
5. Lack of attention by parents to the moral education of children, and shortcomings such as showing a bad temper, estrangement, disputes, anger, slander, and so on.
6. The use of alcohol in families.
7. The addiction of the father or mother to smoking.
8. Unsuitable associates of one or both parents.

Even the number and the type of books in a home, the level of education of the mother, and the way the ts talk to each other, have a bearing on the child's psychological make-up.

Lesgaft, (a Russian specialist in the study of children's characters, he was considered one of the distinguished intellectuals of his age) identified six different effects produced in children by the family environment.

1. If the children of a family are paid no attention and ignored by the parents, if they are accorded no importance whatsoever, but are belittled and looked on with contempt, and if no effort is put into their training and education, they will develop into hypocrites and liars, and their mental growth will be impaired and very slow.

2. If parents are always admiring their children and praising them when the children themselves are present, then the children become selfish, superficial, complacent, and lacking in originality.

3. In families whose lives are relaxed and happy, and where sincere love and true harmony exist between the parents, the children grow up to be kind-hearted, their power of thought is intense, and they have an extreme love of learning.

4. If parents are not fair-minded and object to everything the children do, constantly criticizing and finding fault, the children will become completely fed up with their families, while at the bottom of their hearts will always remain a residue of anger and resentment. These children are also excitable, and the slightest thing makes them nervous.

5. If parents pamper children excessively, hovering over and treating them like babies irrespective of their

ages, not even wanting to see them put on their own shoes, then the children, by being withheld from all physical and mental activity, will become idle, and will always be afraid to face the realities of life.

6. In families where extreme poverty exists, but the love of the parents is nevertheless evident, the children as they grow will become hard-working, calm, obedient, and humble. But if economic hardship is combined with parental unkindness and bad disposition, then the children of that family become miserable, debilitated, and forlorn. They always view the present and future with mixed feelings of disappointment and hopelessness.

We can see how extensive is the influence which families have on the mentality of children; that the foundation of the morals, the manner of behaviour, and the social life of children are, in truth, based on the family structure; that the happiness or misery – and, as a result, the progress – of society depends on the words, actions, care, and attention of the mothers and fathers. Clearly, the parents – and especially the mother – should realize fully the extent of their noble responsibilities. Whatever actions they undertake, whatever words they utter, whomsoever they associate with, whatever tasks they may resolve to do, they must always keep before their eyes the sacred duties which devolve upon them as parents. Treading this path is not as easy as one might be inclined to think, and the wayfarer setting out on the journey should provide himself liberally with patience, forbearance, steadfastness, ceaseless endeavour, knowledge, and perception.

The Responsibility of the Mother

The task of bringing up a Bahá'í child, as emphasized time and again in the Bahá'í writings, is the chief responsibility of the mother, whose unique privilege is indeed to create in her home such conditions as would be most conducive to both his material and spiritual welfare and advancement. The training which a child first receives through his mother constitutes the strongest foundation for his future development . . .[2]

O ye loving mothers, know ye that in God's sight, the best of all ways to worship Him is to educate the children and train them in all the perfections of humankind; and no nobler deed than this can be imagined.[3]

The duties and responsibilities of the mother of the family are, of course, more demanding than those of the father. It is the mother who sets the moral standards of her children and establishes their conduct. Since she is the constant companion of her children, her beliefs, thoughts, opinions, conduct, and habits are easily transferred to them. The mother should, therefore, in all affairs and under all conditions, carefully assess her behaviour, and not overstep sound educational bounds for even a second; she should strive to demonstrate maturity and praiseworthy characteristics, so that her children may regard her as their example and follow in her footsteps. If, God forbid, the dignity of the mother should lessen in the eyes of the children, and respect for the lofty station of motherhood cease to exist, then the task of training will be very difficult or even impossible.

It is clear that the father, too, should always keep this important point in mind, and never belittle the

mother or do anything which might decrease her wo
in the eyes of the children. The weakening of the
station of motherhood constitutes a lethal blow to the
well-being of children, destroying the foundation of
the family unit. So important is this principle of training that, of all subjects dealing with education, it is
outranked by none.

The Importance of a Close Relationship between Parents and Children

*Ye should consider the question of goodly character as
of the first importance. It is incumbent upon every father
and mother to counsel their children over a long period,
and guide them unto those things which lead to everlasting honour.*[4]

Many fathers limit their duties at home to looking
after the material well-being of their families, while
outside the home, their jobs are the focal points of
their lives; this attitude is usually coupled with a lack
of interest in those spiritual matters essential to every
family. Following the same pattern, many mothers
concentrate their efforts at home on providing meals
and looking after the day to day requirements, while
paying scant attention to fostering the spiritual and
intellectual capacities of their children. They leave this
most important of responsibilities entirely in the hands
of kindergartens, elementary schools and boarding
schools.

Many parents, therefore, do not develop a close and
friendly relationship with their offspring – almost as
though they considered companionship with them to
be below the station of adults. They rapidly become
annoyed by their children's loud voices, laughter and

talkativeness; they tell them frankly, 'Leave us in peace so we can get on with our work.' This pattern of thinking is an absolute mistake, and the methods used are totally erroneous, for the best place to foster an attitude of kind-heartedness, healthy emotions and right thinking in children is the home, and the most qualified educators are the fathers and mothers. Never can kindergartens or schools replace the home, no matter how perfectly these institutions may function.

'With reference to the question of the training of children,' wrote Shoghi Effendi, 'given the emphasis placed by Bahá'u'lláh and 'Abdu'l-Bahá on the necessity for the parents to train their children while still in their tender age, it would seem preferable that they should receive their first training at home at the hand of their mother, rather than be sent to a nursery. Should circumstances, however, compel a Bahá'í mother to adopt the latter course, there can be no objection.'[5]

It is the nature of kindergartens and elementary schools to treat all their pupils in virtually the same way. The methods of teaching and instruction are almost identical for everyone; one set programme applies to all students. Even if these institutions wanted to arrange their classes taking into account the differing characteristics, whether inborn or acquired, of each child, they would find it next to impossible, for, in spite of the marvellous progress which has been achieved in the science of education, the question of individuality has, by and large, remained unsolved. Experts have been unable to delve so thoroughly into the underlying principles of education as to be able to

take into account the exigencies of every child
deal with his particular needs. The writer has
many kindergartens and schools in Europe, ha
sonally taught and instructed students, and has found
that specialists in this field admit their incapacity to
deal with the subject.

We are obliged to confess, therefore, that the influence exerted by the family on the course which the
education of children takes is not to be regarded as an
insignificant matter. The mothers who have reared
their children and are familiar with all their sentiments,
feelings, manners, and inclinations, are in the best
position to direct and guide them. For this reason,
mothers should be encouraged to stay with their young
children, especially in the early years, rather than go
out to work and have to leave their children with a
baby-sitter or at the kindergarten. Careful organization, the making of personal sacrifices and the acquisition of a certain amount of technical knowledge are,
of course, essential.

Many of the complicated problems involved in the
training of children can be solved at home if the
parents will seek to establish a close relationship with
them, play the part of their true friends and companions, listen to their childish talk, and try, using wise
and easily-understood language, to rectify their shortcomings. In families where this indispensable matter
has been considered carefully, a specific time is often
set aside for talking with the children. During this
time, the parents and children sit together in a circle
and discuss a different topic on each occasion. Sometimes the parents tell stories; at other times, they

encourage the children to speak. Some of the most intricate educational problems can be resolved during these moments of conversation and companionship.

Friendship between Mothers and Children

For mothers are the first educators, the first mentors; and truly it is the mothers who determine the happiness, the future greatness, the courteous ways and learning and judgement, the understanding and the faith of their little ones.[6]

Children are always in need of someone with whom to share their thoughts and worries: they need the guidance and assistance of an affectionate friend. A complete and abiding friendship between a mother and her child can never be over-estimated. A young child should be able to see his mother as a faithful friend, an intimate companion, and a source of refuge, confiding in her in all matters and keeping nothing hidden from her.

If the mother is not regarded in this light, the child will have no option but to find somebody else to fill this position; he will look up to that person in a friendly and trusting manner, willingly offering him the key to his heart. Such will be the degree of influence enjoyed by his friend that the child will feel submissive and subservient to him, treasuring in his heart whatever the friend may say. Such a situation poses a dangerous threat to the young child, for his friend – like himself – is inexperienced and lacking in sound judgement. It is all too evident what sorrowful and detrimental consequences will result if neither the guide nor the guided can distinguish a path from a precipice, or a thief from a nightwatchman.

Despite this, and for various reasons, some mothers bestow not the least bit of attention or affection on their children. Instead of making them enamoured with kindness, these parents usually appear to be tired of seeing their children, although this impression may not reflect their true sentiments. But the effect, all the same, is to make intimacy and companionship impossible. And the children, for their part, avoid the coldness of their mothers, and turn to other people. They unload their hearts on inexperienced friends, placing their destinies in the hands of people like themselves, and cherishing whatever advice they may receive in return.

For example: A seven-year-old child witnesses some incident or overhears some comments which puzzle him; he becomes obsessed with finding an explanation, and concentrates his full attention on it. But he finds himself unable to unravel the problem by himself. It occurs to him that his mother is the best person to ask. He quickly walks home, and in a state of unconcealed joy goes straight to his mother, presents her with the problem, and asks for help. But the mother, weary from housework, is busy preparing lunch, and says that she is feeling nervous and has butterflies in her stomach. She has neither the time nor the patience for the child and says harshly, 'Can't you see that I'm up to my neck in work? I don't have any time for your chatter. What's all this gibberish?'

The reaction of the mother so disheartens the child that he slinks away and vows never again to ask her to explain anything. His curiosity, however, remains unsatisfied, and dominates his entire being. Inevitably, he thinks of another approach, and elects to share the matter with a friend who sits next to him in class. At the first opportunity, he presents the question, and his schoolmate gives an answer which suits his taste and understanding. Perhaps that piece of 'advice' will haunt and fetter him throughout his life, whereas if the mother had paid even a little attention to his query and reacted properly, he would not have gone to his uninformed friend for help, and the course of his life would have been significantly different.

Scholars have long since discovered the importance of true friendship between mother and child. How to talk to a child has become an educational technique in itself, and is a course of study in the science of education. Among the books available on this subject can be mentioned the writings of Ort, a Dutch author who was one of the first to recommend question and answer exchanges for solving the problems children think up. Parents would do well to read some of these books. According to their capacity, they should give convincing and satisfying answers to their child, and always provide him with an opportunity for conversation and asking questions. The bonds of friendship and affection should never be severed by rough treatment; any actions which might keep the child aloof from his mother should be avoided. In this way, the child will regard his mother as a never-failing source of love and affection, will share his thoughts and anxieties with her, and not flee from her presence.

The Consequences of Neglecting Children's Training

O maid-servants of the Merciful! It is incumbent upon you to train the children from their earliest babyhood! It is incumbent upon you to beautify their morals! It is incumbent upon you to attend to them under all aspects and circumstances, inasmuch as God – glorified and exalted is He! – hath ordained mothers to be the primary trainers of children and infants. This is a great and important affair and a high and exalted position, and it is not allowable to slacken therein at all![7]

The sacred duty which devolves upon mothers is of such importance that they should permit nothing whatever to impede its realization. Otherwise, the edifice of human happiness will be defaced, and mankind will succumb to various ills. Whoever has been blessed with the distinguished station of parenthood should set as his primary objective the refinement of the morals and conduct of his children.

Needless to say, it has been observed that many parents are oblivious of this, their most important duty, and allow the seriousness of their responsibilities to fade from their sight. Much of the precious time which should be dedicated to the training and refinement of their children is spent on non-essentials; every trifling matter is given preference to the fostering of the children's education and development. Only during moments of leisure do they remember their distressed children, and, with total indifference, enquire into their condition. They will even occasionally issue ludicrous and meaningless instructions to the children, while remaining completely unaware of their physical and spiritual requirements.

For example: A mother has gone to bed late, and as a result she does not get up in the morning until after the children have prepared their own breakfasts and got themselves ready for school. If young children –

who always stand in need of supervision – are deprived of the care and attention of the mother, and if they find themselves free, independent, and unrestrained, they will grow as weeds do, without acquiring commendable characteristics. They may, for instance, forget to wash their hands and faces and brush their teeth – duties which are essential to good health; also, they may neglect to say prayers. At breakfast, they may not eat enough and later, perhaps they will not dress in a proper and orderly manner. As a result of this lack of care, they head off to school in a truly deplorable state. And when they return home, they do not see the mother, for she has gone to select material to take to the dressmaker, leaving them to prepare and eat lunch on their own. These children's predicament can be likened to that of a moving car whose steering has been abandoned by the driver.

In the late afternoon, the children return from school in time to see the mother preparing to go out. From her stance in front of the mirror, she gives 'motherly' advice, and with the utmost 'kindness' and 'compassion' says: 'My darling children, your father and I are invited out for the evening and we may not be back until late. Do your homework, behave yourselves, and don't bother the baby-sitter. After you have supper, please go to bed early.'

If one of the children has the courage to object to the mother's habit of always leaving them alone, she pounces on that child like a roaring lion with, 'Bravo! And when did you become my boss? When did children start interfering in the business of grown-ups? You are out all day. You go to school, you play with other children. But I don't go anywhere, and now that we are invited out, Your Majesty thinks that I should sit at home for his sake. What kind of thing is that to say?' The mother inflicts so many of these 'counsels' on the poor child that he feels as though he has been raked over the coals, and regrets his 'rudeness' a thousand times over.

When the parents return from the visit, the children have long since gone to sleep. A family environment of this nature can be compared to an orchard which has no gardener to water and care for the tender saplings; it will, of course, cease to be productive or pleasing to the eye, and before long, its trees will become dry wood, fit only for the fire.

The mothers should, therefore, make every sacrifice for the education of their beloved children. They should subordinate every personal liking and want to the happiness of their children; no other goal should supersede that of the training and refinement of their offspring. They should know that no one else, be it helpers, nannies, baby-sitters, or even relatives, can perform this all-important task which the Almighty has conferred upon mothers.

Those parents who foolishly ignore their child-raising responsibilities will find that when their children grow and develop into coarse individuals, devoid of human virtues, the first to suffer the consequences will be the mothers and fathers themselves. Later, other members of society will be affected too.

Safeguarding the Dignity of the Mother

Whensoever a mother seeth that her child hath done well, let her praise and applaud him and cheer his heart; and if the slightest undesirable trait should manifest itself, let her counsel the child and punish him, and use means based on reason, even a slight verbal chastisement should this be necessary.[8]

Just as a mother is merciful, kind and compassionate, and always converses with her child in warm and affectionate language, preferring the use of words as mild as milk to harsh language which cuts the delicate heart of the child like a sword – so too, she must take adequate precautions to safeguard her own dignity. She should never belittle herself when dealing with children, or give in to a child's improper demands. If the mother refuses to submit to his stubbornness and selfishness, the child will in turn dismiss the idea that his mother is afraid of him, that she is obedient to his orders and demands, that whatever he says is acceptable, and that nobody is able to withstand his determination.

This matter is so vital in the family that, in the opinion of the writer, the parents should never permit the worth of the mother to be impaired; for if her lofty station declines in the sight of the offspring, the organization of the family will be reduced to shambles, and chaos will prevail within that small 'country' to such a degree that no force will be able to re-establish peace and tranquillity.

The mother should not use authoritarian, cruel or illogical measures to maintain her dignity and station but neither should she submit to the unreasonable demands of the child. She must tread the path of moderation and avoid these two extremes. The poet Sa'di wrote:

A blend of love and discipline,
this is the golden mean;
like the art of the blood-letter
who hurts but to heal.

If a mother's dignity is lowered in the eyes of her child, and she becomes his laughing-stock, no ray of hope will remain of training him.

Picture this scene (all these examples have actually occurred; they are not merely products of the imagination) in which a five-year-old child wakes up and no sooner opens his eyes than he starts crying and calls out to his mother in a demanding way. The moment the mother hears the child, she rushes to his side to see what he wants. She talks to him in a humble manner, asking: 'What would you like, darling? Won't you get up and come and have your breakfast?' The child, still lying down, raises his eyebrows and continues crying. He says, 'I don't want to get out of bed. Bring me my breakfast so I can have it here.' His attitude worries the mother; speaking with the utmost meekness, like a captive to a conqueror, she replies: 'But my dear, you have to wash your hands and face and then come to the table and have your breakfast. Please get up, my little darling.'

Once again the child takes the offensive and screams, 'I said I'm not going to get up. Hurry up and bring my breakfast here.' The mother is hesitant to carry out his demand, but the child overcomes her resistance by kicking and hollering. She gives in to his wishes and says, 'All right, all right. Don't cry. I'll bring breakfast to you right now.'

After a few minutes the mother appears, carrying a tray of food in her hands; she is granted permission to enter His Majesty's chamber, and offers him his morning meal.

To relate every detail of this situation would substantially lengthen this short description. Briefly, the child issues orders out of ignorance and lack of proper discipline, and the mother reduced to a state of helplessness and submissiveness, obeys him and carries them out.

At lunch time, the child lords it over the mother to such an extent as to arouse pity in an impartial observer. When, for instance, the little boy wants water, he does not demean himself by stretching out his hand and pouring his own from the crystal pitcher which is right in front of his eyes, but instead, he chooses to point his index finger at the glass in order to make his mother understand – without a single word being spoken – that he is thirsty. Woe betide the mother if she fails to grasp his intention and neglects to pour the water, for his selfish shouts and screams will resound throughout the room, and again he will point disdainfully towards the empty glass. This time, the mother reacts as if she had just awakened from a trance, and says: 'Do you want some water, my darling? All right, I'm sorry, I hadn't noticed that your glass was empty. Here is some water for you.'

A child like this controls his mother as he would a puppet, whatever his heart desires will be realized. Such scenes I have often witnessed with feelings of amazement and regret, but out of courtesy and respect, I have never permitted myself to interfere in other people's affairs.

On one occasion (when I was present) a young child shouted at his mother, 'Leave me alone and go out of this room and let me do what I want to.' The mother hesitated a moment, and then tried to dissuade the child from his intentions, but she remained in the room. The child then went and bruised the mother's body by pinching her. Yet the mother continued talking to him all the time in an over-affectionate manner.

The point is this: neither harshness, anger, and authoritarian measures taken by the mother, nor her belittlement, helplessness and incapacity in the sight of the children, are acceptable. Kindness and compassion should be combined with perfect prudence, reason, dignity and self-respect, so that moderation prevails.

Contributions of the Father

The youth must grow and develop and take the place of their fathers.[9]

. . . no matter how urgent and vital the requirements of the teaching work may be, you should under no circumstances neglect the education of your children, as towards them you have an obligation no less sacred than towards the Cause.[10]

'How could such excellent parents have raised such terrible children?' is an oft-repeated question asked by the dumbfounded friends and relatives of a family where the parents are the embodiments of good morals and exemplary conduct, and have rendered noteworthy services to their fellow man, but whose children, upon reaching maturity, have lived very different lives, and their behaviour disgraced their families.

'The treasure is gone, replaced by a snake.'

Since there exists a definite cause of every effect in this world, so too this puzzling subject has its explanations.

1. The parents, but more especially the fathers, neither take note of the conduct of their children nor pay sufficient attention to their training. Most of these fathers' free time is spent outside the home in the service of society, while no time is devoted to their own families. They return home, tired and weary, for the sole purpose of resting and replenishing their energy, for these fathers are of the belief that serving society requires that they be away from their families most of the time.

When the mother is left on her own to care for the children, and is deprived of the assistance and co-operation of the father who has an important influence on the children's (and especially the boys') training, then that household will be in a position similar to that of a person trying to stand on one foot.

For example, a father has just returned home after completing his day at work. He spends a few moments reading, and then goes for a short walk to refresh himself. He returns, has supper with the family, and immediately goes out to attend some social function. He comes back with enough time on his hands to do some reading and writing before going to bed.

Will this family and these children have any real existence for such a father? Will he have any influence on the training and education of his offspring? This father hardly has time to talk to his children; he rarely enquires into their condition, or concerns himself with the guidance which they so direly need. He may be compared to a host who is too reserved to talk with his guests. How is it possible for a father in such circumstances to protect his children from the numberless forms of physical and mental anguish, and guide them correctly? Such a father may be of benefit to others, and may make precious contributions to society through his lectures and articles, but these things will bear little or no fruit in his own family.

The father who pays little attention to his children, dedicating all his time to other interests outside the home, has erred seriously. The hardship sustained and the efforts made in the spirit of service by this industrious father regrettably produce nothing but trouble for his family; if others remember him for his good deeds, his children remember his neglect; their disconcerting behaviour will dishonour him, and in the next world he will be called to account for his failure to discharge his responsibilities.

It is therefore essential that fathers do not neglect in the least this all-important matter. As their first duty, they must attend to their children and, according to their means, provide for their training and education. Any free time can then be used for social work.

2. This point concerns the lack of attention given by the father to his children's activities outside the home, and is a direct result of the first point. Such fathers do not often know whom their children associate with, and what they do for recreation and amusement.

There can be no doubt that a father who remains unaware of the state of his children within the family environment will remain unaware of their conduct outside the family as well. And it is as clear as the light of day that no matter how noble a child may be by nature, when he is deprived of parental guidance and supervision he will deviate from the right path and direct himself towards discreditable deeds.

It is not my intention to dissuade fathers from contributing to the betterment of their fellow man, but rather to point out that such dedicated individuals should first consider their families and concentrate on the training and education of their children. These are by far their greater responsibilities. Afterwards, as time permits, they can attend to their social commitments.

The Difficult Years

The youth, in particular, must constantly and determinedly strive to exemplify a Bahá'í life. In the world around us we see moral decay, promiscuity, indecency, vulgarity, bad manners – the Bahá'í young people must be the opposite of these things, and, by their chastity, their uprightness, their decency, their consideration and good manners, attract others, old and young, to the Faith. The world is tired of words; it wants example, and it is up to the Bahá'í youth to furnish it.[11]

Parents usually express satisfaction with their pre-adolescent children. They get along more or less in peace and happiness; rarely does estrangement occur between them. During these years, the parent-child relationship is quite clear: the parents are the governors, and the children are the governed; the fathers and mothers pass the laws, and the children obey them.

But beginning at the age of twelve or thirteen, and continuing until seventeen or eighteen, this relationship alters drastically. Discontent gradually rears its head on both sides, and feelings of estrangement conceal the underlying affection. The attitudes of adolescents change towards their parents; little by little they resort to fault-finding and other forms of criticism; they often become quick-tempered. The family environment no longer suits their tastes, and their restlessness creates a rift between the parents and themselves.

If we reflect for a moment on this matter, we will see that the most difficult stage of life from the viewpoint of training and education is this very period. Specialists refer to it as the age of transformation, for it is at this age that great changes, both external and internal, occur in children. Some of these changes are obvious, while others are concealed. For instance, children's voices change noticeably at this time, and their growth is rapid; special glands which have lain dormant now begin functioning. Occurring simultaneously with these bodily changes are changes in the intellect, as totally new feelings, inclinations, and demands begin to appear. Adolescents see themselves in a different world; they are often at a loss to clarify their new identity, having shed the last remnants of childhood, but not yet having attained complete maturity. The ship of their beings has detached itself from one shore, but has not yet arrived at the other. They are neither boys nor men, neither girls nor women. Signs of a lack of perseverence and instability characterize the actions of the adolescent. At times, he hides away from everyone and remains cooped up in his room; at other times, he spends hours with acquaintances and friends, enjoying himself totally. On some occasions he is so overcome with feelings of lethargy that he cannot summon up the patience to perform the ritual of washing his hands and face, but on other occasions, he can hardly contain his eagerness as he busies himself with various projects.

There is also an overpowering desire at this age to be regarded as a mature adult, as somebody to be looked up to. Attempts to model himself on grown-ups sometimes lead him to use harsh language and to be short-tempered. He often tries to make others obey his orders, but at the same time, he avoids listening to other people.

If parents can readily recognize the signs of puberty and adolescence; if they base their relationship with adolescents on strong principles of education, and if they do not treat them in the same manner as they treated them in childhood, then they will be much more capable of training their mental and physical faculties. They will be able to follow a methodical route, instead of wandering aimlessly in a wilderness of doubt.

Since this facet of training is of extreme importance, I should like to draw parents' attention to the following points.

1. The temperament of an adolescent is usually unstable and liable to quick changes. His moods rarely stay within the bounds of moderation; this is accompanied by a general dissatisfaction with existing conditions, and by an inner turmoil. His demands are more often than not ambiguous even to himself, and his budding imagination is darkened by doubt. He often finds himself searching for something the nature of

which even he cannot define. Most of the time h
himself as lonely and solitary. He is afraid, and
to find a kind friend on whom to unload his sor
His goals, thoughts, and emotions are quite different
from those experienced during childhood. If, for instance, collecting stamps used to give him joy, suddenly this source of pleasure becomes meaningless,
uninteresting, and even abhorrent. That same boy who
was happy to play and run with his age-mates, and that
same girl who used to spend her time with dolls, today
feel attracted to more serious things, and to the consideration of intellectual matters.

Given these new developments, parents would be
wise to provide their children with a helping hand, and
by using their experience, discretion, and intelligence,
protect their offspring from this mental anguish. This
means that the father and mother should, as far as they
are able, spend their free time at home. Instead of
tidying up odds and ends – finishing the office work,
balancing the budget, doing the housework, and the
like – they ought to be with their adolescent children,
and discuss their feelings and state of mind with them
in a courteous and friendly manner (as expected from
affectionate mothers and fathers), and not leave them
to themselves. To become their unstinting friends and
compassionate companions; to help them in times of
peril; to give them any necessary advice; to direct and
guide them; to go out together; to converse on a
friendly level; to assist them in selecting a field of
study, in starting a business, and so on, and to obtain,
if need be, the assistance of experienced people in this
undertaking; to become in reality their counsellors and
advisors, and not create a gap between themselves and

their offspring – these are the things parents should try to do, so that the rapidly maturing children, as a result of their parents' counsels and recognizing the sincerity of their friendship, may overcome their own doubts, perplexity, loneliness, and isolation, and, distinguishing clearly between the right and wrong path, joyfully choose the one which confers happiness. Reaching their final destination, they will understand the meaning of the verse,

> Turn not away, O youth,
> from an elder's considered advice;
> for his counsel is often better
> than taking a chance on luck.

However talented, capable, intelligent, and strong they may be, adolescents are in need of the advice of their more experienced parents as provision for the often hazardous journey of life lying ahead.

2. Adolescents want to understand everything. Their intellectual faculties, especially the memory, intensify greatly, and their imaginations are correspondingly strengthened. The personality manifests itself more and more, and the word 'I' is used frequently. Unlike children, adolescents care a great deal about their appearance, paying an increasing amount of attention to the style of their clothing, and taking care not to be criticized by others. This self-awareness sometimes leads to an exaggerated self-esteem. As they do not want to be defeated (in their view) by other people, they tend to insist on their own opinions.

The reading of some kinds of stories often leads adolescents to want to depict themselves in the role of the heroes and heroines, and attempts at imitation often result in serious blows to their pride. This removes the adolescent far from the world of reality and takes him into the realm of fancies and abstractions, leaving him with his head in the clouds, sailing on the wings of imagination. When children are going through this stage in their development, parents should treat them with the utmost kindness and compassion, and should shun the use of unpleasant or ugly words. They should never belittle them in front of others, but adhere to reasoning when explaining things or discussing problems. In this way, adolescents will understand perfectly the logic behind their parents' explanations, and will not become rude and obstinate. For just as the heart should be receptive to words, so the words should be pleasing to the heart.

Parents should no longer treat their offspring as though they were still children, nor should they converse with them in a childish manner. Rather, they should consult them on all matters; the use of harsh words should be avoided, and their actions should be characterized by courtesy. Parents should be aware that any coarse or rude behaviour which their children may manifest at this age is of a temporary nature, and will pass. At appropriate times, of course, the parents should advise and counsel their children sympathetically, making them understand that such behaviour and conduct are unbecoming and that they should try to shun it. If older people show respect for youth and treat them considerately, they will safeguard respect for themselves.

Parents should also be ready to accept the legitimate and logical demands of their children, and, if they can afford it, provide them with recreational or educational equipment. In this way, the children will turn their backs on street attractions, and acquire an affection for the home environment. Also, parents ought to answer their questions as capably as they can, to approve anything which they express correctly and soundly, to satisfy completely any feelings of curiosity, and, above all, to create in them an understanding of the status enjoyed by the mother and father. This will, in turn, make them well aware that respect for parents and obedience to them are the foundation of morality and good behaviour. If adolescents fully understand this point, one of the many doors to happiness will open before them, and they will find themselves protected from various difficulties. It can be said that if love for the parents permeates the very hearts of adolescents, it will act as a shield to protect them from the poisonous darts hurled by the foes of morality. Of course, this important goal depends to no small degree on the nature of the relationship which exists between parents and their maturing children, for adolescents should be treated in such a way that they will act naturally towards their parents with perfect politeness, dignity, humility, and courtesy. They should know and understand that their happiness both in this world and the next lies in the blessings and consent of their parents. They should be so united with them that they can say,

Consumed in fiery torment with you,
preferable to being with others
in Paradise.

Consultation with Adolescents

. . . true consultation is spiritual conference in the attitude and atmosphere of love.[12]

One day I happened to talk to an eighteen-year-old youth, and as we knew each other from previous encounters, I asked how life was treating him. Without the least hesitation, he unloosed a flood of complaints and expressed deep dissatisfaction about the behaviour of his parents, whom he considered the main cause of his unhappiness. When I became more fully informed about the matter, and found out the reasons for such impoverished thinking, I realized that this young man, not unlike many of his peers, had erred seriously, and that the wisdom and perception of his parents were in sharp contrast with his own hasty judgement. Analysing the matter further, however, I became convinced that his father and mother had not exactly dealt with their child according to sound principles of training and education, and had unintentionally contributed to his present state of mind.

The boy had given me this account:

'Whenever I want to say something at home – express an opinion or talk about my future – Mum and Dad immediately interrupt and silence me in no uncertain terms. Then, in my absence, they make decisions, and subsequently insist that I carry them out. Since I do not consider those decisions to be enforceable, and do not agree with them, I am not willing to obey them. And if I pretend to be obedient and go along with their decisions, I show my objections in other ways, and begin to feel hatred towards my parents in my heart.'

Comments of this nature help us recognize more clearly the need for consultation in a family. When children reach adolescence, all matters concerning them should be patiently and painstakingly discussed, so that an understanding may be reached. Through consultation with their helpful and more experienced parents, adolescents are able to see the different facets of the subject under discussion. Becoming aware of the various problems involved and appraising them, they will find no excuse to complain, will avoid quarrelling with their parents, and, in later years, will not shed tears of regret over deplorable deeds committed in the past.

Whenever a problem involving adolescent children in the family arises, a discussion aimed at devising a solution should immediately take place, and the mother, father, and other adult members of the household should be present. The adolescents themselves should take part in the consultation and express their opinions and views. If, during the consultation, immature comments are put forward by the adolescents present, indicating an inclination to follow a non-moderate path, the parents should correct them kindly and through the use of sound reasoning. Usually the children will then dispense with their unreasonable views. But if they remain unconvinced, the parents, after careful deliberation, should state the course of action they recommend, and point out to their adolescent children that they will undoubtedly come to acknowledge the wisdom behind the decision as time goes on.

This approach will have a number of beneficial results:

1. The principle of consultation is one of the fundamental elements of the divine edifice, and through the use of this method its foundation will be firmly established in families.

2. By acquiring the habit of consulting and deliberating on important matters from an early age, adolescents will develop into sociable individuals, capable of deep thinking.

3. The parents, more than before, will take into consideration the feelings, emotions, and needs of their children, and learn their intentions, for it is through the exchange of thoughts and views that the truth is to some extent discovered.

4. Adolescents will no longer feel inclined to the view that unjust orders have been issued by authoritarian parents without any consideration given to their wishes and requests.

5. The rapidly-maturing children will come to grasp the complexities of the problems under discussion, and, through understanding and perception, will willingly submit to any decisions arrived at.

In the full knowledge that consultation will bear good results, I strongly recommend that all questions and problems which may arise in families be settled in this way.

8

TRAINING CHILDREN IN THE SPIRIT OF RELIGION

*For every praiseworthy deed is born out of the light of re-
ligion, and lacking this supreme bestowal the child will
not turn away from any evil, nor will he draw nigh to any
good.*[1]

*Among these children many blessed souls will arise, if
they be trained according to the Bahá'í Teachings.*[2]

PRESENT-DAY PARENTS and educators often do not give
this subject the attention it deserves. Yet experience
has proven beyond doubt that man's best shield against
the darts of temptations is the fear of God. For man
possesses two natures: his spiritual or higher nature,
and his material or lower nature. If his spiritual nature
is trained and developed, he will attain the noblest of
stations in the world of humanity; if he is deprived of
divine education, he will be no better than an animal.
'Were there no educator, all souls would remain
savage,'[3] wrote 'Abdu'l-Bahá, and he explained,
'Close investigation will show that the primary cause
of oppression and injustice, of unrighteousness, irregu-
larity and disorder, is the people's lack of religious
faith and the fact that they are uneducated.'[4]

Only religion has the capacity to free man from his
lower nature and establish a firm and solid rampart
against animal desires; it conquers his inclination for

wrongdoing, and makes the animal nature subservient to the spiritual, safeguarding him from committing whatever is unbefitting.

Childhood is the most appropriate time for fostering the spiritual nature of man and establishing attitudes of true worship and devoutness, for sowing the seeds of faith, and upholding the station of religion – the true source of all divine attributes and perfections. The educator who can best assume such a sacred responsibility is the mother. Naturally she herself should be a worshipper of the true God and be devout in the real sense of the word. She should not disregard the punishment and retribution of the next world, as adumbrated in the Scriptures; she should continually illumine her heart with the light of faith and certitude, and should acknowledge and believe sincerely in the All-Glorious Lord, so that the same true spirit of religion, free from all outward trappings and bigotry, may be instilled in the hearts of her precious children. Through the use of stories and examples, and in simple language, mothers should explain these matters to their children from the time that the children are able to understand them.

At appropriate times, the mother should little by little help her child with basic religious concepts. There is one God, the Creator of this world, Who has brought life into being and Who provides us with our daily bread. Through His prophets He has guided and directed us towards the correct path. He is the All-Knowing, the All-Wise. Not only is He aware of our words and deeds, but He knows our inner secrets. Nothing remains hidden from His sight.

He accompanies us in our loneliness and solitude, and is with us at all times. Every act we do, every word we utter, and every thought that may occur to our minds is known to God, and we should be certain of this. Perhaps we are able to conceal things from each other, but we can never hide them from God, for He is aware of everything, and He is the All-Powerful . . .

The method of presenting these realities, however, depends on the needs, the age, the level of under-standing and the capacity of the child. A young child, for instance, may repeatedly raise a particular matter related to this topic which he wants explained. Then the mother, relying on her God-given intelligence, should clothe the subject with examples and parables, and depict it clearly for her child. If she is unable to do this by herself, she should refer to books which have been written for the purpose, or obtain the assistance of persons who are more experienced and better informed.

In short, this meritorious undertaking should be put into practice in any way suitable, so that the worship of God and the teachings of religion may be gradually instilled in children. To be negligent in this matter is to deal a fatal blow to the souls and bodies of children, for as a result, tumultuous storms of transgressions will uproot those subtle and fresh plants.

A person who has not in childhood been taught piety and the principles of religion, in whom the fear of God has not been inculcated, and whose heart has not been illumined with the light of faith will, in many cases, not shun odious actions, nor turn away from the violation of high moral codes. For individuals who concern themselves only with material comforts and sensual pleasures while paying scant attention to matters pertaining to the soul, and ignoring punishment and retribution, are like totally inexperienced novices mounted on wild horses. It is not difficult to envisage the destinies of such people.

Every important undertaking naturally entails varying degrees of hardship, and man cannot – and morally does not have the right to – evade his responsibilities solely for the sake of freeing himself from trouble. True education of children is, of course, an arduous task, and the educator must, physically and spiritually, endure the hardship, the suffering and the toil which are required. Mothers and fathers alike must bear these hardships willingly, for the sake of their children's future happiness.

Fear of God

We have admonished Our loved ones to fear God, a fear which is the fountainhead of all goodly deeds and virtues. It is the commander of the hosts of justice in the city of Bahá. Happy the man that hath entered the shadow of its luminous standard, and laid fast hold thereon.[5]

O people of God! That which traineth the world is Justice, for it is upheld by two pillars, reward and punishment. These two pillars are the sources of life to the world.[6]

Parents are aware that all the divinely-revealed books tell of the Unseen, Inaccessible and Unknowable God, Who has created all things. He is the Most Great, the All-Powerful, the All-Pervasive; nothing escapes His knowledge. All followers of the divine religions regard these beliefs as the indispensable foundation of their spiritual growth. To expand on this theme now would take us far from our main purpose; but here are a few quotations related to the principal subject.

In the Qur'án we read, 'The eyes attain Him not, but He attains the eyes. He is the All-Subtle, the All-Aware.' (6:103.) And later, 'He knows the treachery of the eyes and what the breasts conceal.' (40:20.)

The fear of God derives from these beliefs. It constitutes the main pillar of religion; the believer who sees God as omnipresent is certain that his words and deeds, whether good or bad, are known to God and that no action will remain without its due reward or punishment.

The fear of God is a prime factor in education. Whoever inculcates in his heart the fear of God – in other words, he whose conscience keeps him alert – will shun an infinity of odious actions. For this reason, this matter has been emphasized in the Scriptures; for example, in the Book of Proverbs in the Old Testament: ' . . . fear the Lord, and depart from evil.' (3:7.) 'The fear of the Lord prolongeth days.' (10:27.) 'He that walketh in his uprightness feareth the Lord: but he that is perverse in his ways despiseth him.' (14:2.) 'The eyes of the Lord are in every place beholding the evil and the good.' (15:3.) 'By humility and the fear of the Lord are riches, and honour, and life.' (22:4.)

And also, in the 'Words of Wisdom' of Bahá'u'lláh: 'The essence of wisdom is the fear of God.'

The Qur'án points out that the fear of God is one of the chief characteristics of the believer endowed with certitude: 'Surely those who tremble in fear of their Lord . . . those vie in good works.' (23:59.) 'We gave

Moses and Aaron the Salvation and a Radiance, and a Remembrance for the godfearing; such as fear God in the Unseen, trembling because of the Hour.' (21:50.) 'So fear not men, but fear you Me.' (5:48.) And emphasizing even further the importance of this subject: 'If we had sent down this Qur'án upon a mountain, thou wouldst have seen it humbled, split asunder out of the fear of God.' (59:21.)

From this introduction it becomes clear that if educators want children to be trained in the spirit of the religion of God, to shun unpleasant actions as grown-ups, to avoid things prohibited, not to yield to base appetites and not to deviate from the divine exhortations, they must provide the means for the inculcation of the fear of God, and brighten the children's hearts with the light of divine virtue.

In order to achieve this, the mother and father themselves must possess this trait. They must increasingly strengthen the fear of God in their own hearts, through turning towards Him, intoning His words and supplicating at His threshold; they should never approach things forbidden, nor turn their backs on whatever has been commanded. And when the children see their mothers and fathers cleansed from all defilement, when they are educated in the spirit of religion, and when they remain aloof from the corrupting influences of the material world, then the mirrors of their souls will remain unstained by the dust of unworthy deeds, and their consciences will be brightened by the light emanating from good conduct. Happy are the children who spend their childhood with people whose entire beings are free from blameworthy actions; in such homes the angel of divine mercy will shelter those innocent children under its outspread wings.

Parents should also try to draw the attention of their children towards a realization of the greatness, the power and the all-embracing knowledge of the self-subsistent God; they should seize every opportunity to foster this realization in the hearts and souls of their loved ones. When freed from their daily work, the parents should turn the home into a school of divine knowledge, explaining spiritual things in the form of stories, proverbs and examples, in accordance with the capacity and understanding of the children. In addition, the parents themselves should make every effort to broaden their own knowledge so as to be better able to impart these precious pearls of learning to their children. They should use every means at their disposal to ensure that their children are able to understand the following points:

The Creator of the heavens and of the earth is affectionate and kind towards His needy servants. Through His prophets, He has made a distinction between the right path and the path of error, separating good from bad. He has commanded people to do good, and forbidden them even to approach bad deeds. He is ever-watchful over our words and actions; nothing remains hidden from His sight. Our duty is to keep away from anything that He has prohibited, and to turn our faces towards whatever He has commanded, so that He may be pleased with us, for if the Peerless God be not pleased with us, then true happiness will elude us forever.

Backbiting

. . . backbiting quencheth the light of the heart, and extinguisheth the life of the soul.[7]

Backbiting is the name given to that curious act of talking about people who are not present in such a way that they would be gravely offended if they were to learn what was said. Put another way, it means to speak ill of others in their absence. Backbiting is a social disease and spreads like the plague, destroying its victims, extinguishing the flame of love in their hearts, veiling their intellects and harming their souls.

Experience has shown that the lower nature of man strongly inclines him towards this habit; when people are overcome by worldly desires, or by the 'fire of self', they blame others, slander them, spread malicious comments, and backbite – and in so doing, derive from it a form of satisfaction.

In every age, with every fresh outpouring of Divine Grace, the Manifestations of God have explicitly enjoined on everyone the shunning of this behaviour. Well-wishers and promoters of the best interests of civilization, too – advocates of high standards of morality, men of letters, counsellors – have admonished people against fault-finding and backbiting. Such warnings sometimes take the form of counsels or advice; at other times, they are contained in parables. The Qur'án commands: 'And do not backbite one another; would any of you like to eat the flesh of his brother dead?' (42:12.) Here, by comparing backbiting to the eating of human flesh, God Himself admonishes His people against this unspeakably hideous action.

In some of the books of the Old and New Testament, this abominable behaviour has been berated. In Leviticus 19:16 and Proverbs 11:19, backbiters and calumniators are severely reproached. In Matthew 7:4, it is recorded that Christ said: 'Or how wilt thou say to thy brother, Let me pull out the mote out of thine eye; and, behold, a beam is in thine own eye?'

But even though backbiting, fault-finding, and calumny are condemned by all advocates of morality and forbidden in the scriptures, these habits are regrettably still wide-spread in society, and are passed along from generation to generation. For the world to rid itself of this ruinous practice, its remedy must be discovered and adhered to; only then will the sickness cease to be passed from parent to child, and children will be immunized against it from their earliest years.

The best remedy is for the parents themselves to determine to obey the command of God and totally avoid backbiting. In order to protect their loved ones, they must avoid the company of slanderers and gossipers, taking particular care not to speak ill of others when in the presence of children. Even if parents have no control over their behaviour, at least they should not be near children at the time of an outbreak of calumny, for it is clear that the words and actions of parents exert a strong influence on children's behaviour, and that the mother is the prime establisher of a child's morals and conduct. If the flood is dammed up at its source, and the habit does not pass from parents to their children, a strong barrier will have been erected that can halt it completely.

Mothers and fathers should not consider this task impossible or even difficult. Even deeply-ingrained habits can be overcome through the power of determination. A great campaign ought to be conducted to eradicate this misdirected habit, as the longer backbiting goes on in society, the more it will cause unnecessary regret and mental anguish. Those people who, with pure intent, prepare themselves now to enter this arena to play a leading part in such an undertaking are to be all the more commended.

To summarize: children should never hear or see any trace of backbiting or fault-finding in the home. And, since shunning all forms of backbiting conforms with the will of God, then unquestionably those people who make the effort to remove this stain from the mirrors of their hearts will be assisted and strengthened.

Hypocrisy and Dissimulation

Be thou of the people of hell-fire but be not a hypocrite.[8]

Hypocrisy and dissimulation are traits which have been utterly condemned by the Prophets of God, and denounced by many advocates of morality. All have expressed nothing but revulsion for these contemptible qualities, and have pointed out the benefits of removing them from our midst. If an attempt were made to compile all the scriptural verses relevant to this topic, and if these were combined with the considered statements of the learned, they could only be contained within the covers of a large book. What is of interest to us, however, is to discuss this subject from the point of view of education, so that more than ever, parents will recognize the ugly nature of these habits, and will protect and safeguard their children as far as possible from their calamitous effects.

Hypocrisy, dissimulation, two-faced behaviour, and allowing a difference between what is felt in the heart and what is uttered by the tongue are highly contagious spiritual diseases which regrettably pass from generation to generation, from parent to child, leaving their mark on almost everyone. The more these lethal diseases spread, the more devastating are their effects on the foundation of society, and the more intensely do they darken relationships between people. Consider this example:

A father and mother are sitting at home, talking. The children, who have gathered around and are listening to their conversation, notice that the father is criticizing everything about a certain neighbour. 'There is no worse a person in this whole world than our neighbour,' he says. 'He is miserly and cruel. His wife and children suffer continuously. He deprives them of adequate food and clothing. He is so greedy that he spends every moment of the day trying to obtain a few more coins so that he can store them in a corner like worthless stones . . .'

These words are interrupted by a knock on the door, and one of the children, who has been listening very attentively, jumps up and rushes to see who it is. By coincidence, the person who is dropping in for a brief visit is that very same neighbour who was the subject of the discussion between the parents. The innocent children assume that their father will speak angrily to this unwelcome guest, or that, as the host, he will feel obliged to invite the man in but will then act coldly towards him. Words cannot express their surprise as they see both their mother and father speaking with honey-coated tongues as they address the neighbour, and their astonishment is heightened as they listen to their smiling and courteous father saying, 'You are most welcome! We were saying just now that there is no one better in the world than you. You are so generous, your wife and children are comfortable and well taken care of, your home is like paradise, and you yourself are so kind-hearted, providing the best clothes and the best food for your family, and all your work and wealth goes to increase the happiness of your loved ones . . .'

Staring wide-eyed because of this unexpected change, the children cast furtive glances at the mother, the father and at the 'esteemed' guest, but are incapable of solving the puzzle and of abating their bewilderment. Eventually, the guest goes and the situation switches back to its more familiar routine. With even greater anger, the father starts again on the neighbour: 'Did you see how that snake in the grass ate up our time? He is really detestable. If I had my choice, I would never look on his face again; I would move miles away from here . . .'

It is in this way that the seeds of hypocrisy and dissimulation are sown in the hearts and souls of children; during the school years, and later in society, these seeds are watered and grow, until two-faced behaviour becomes second nature to the majority of people, thus leading to the effacement of truthfulness and trustworthiness – two of the strongest pillars of true civilization.

Mothers and fathers alike should therefore strain every nerve to ensure that the hearts of their children remain protected from this most lethal of poisons. The golden rule of training and education is applicable here too: the best method is for the parents themselves to have nothing to do with hypocrisy within the family environment. They must hold themselves aloof from this hateful habit and refuse to allow its noxious vapours to penetrate the home – the place which ought to be consecrated to education and to the acquisition of human perfections. It is essential, moreover, that children be guided towards truthfulness and sincerity under all conditions, for the more wide-spread hypocrisy, deceit, and imposture are in society, the greater will be the decrease in human virtues and excellence, effectively inverting the standards of human happiness and prosperity.

Perseverance is a prerequisite for progress in all matters, and particularly in such important undertakings as those which constitute the pivot of the spiritual regeneration of society. In these cases, unimaginable amounts of patience, forbearance, and endurance are needed. Educators must not, therefore, tire and thereby fail to attain their goal. This matter is indispensable for the proper functioning of society, and can never be taken for granted, inasmuch as serious and ceaseless endeavour is required for its ultimate attainment.

Respect for Parents

There are also certain sacred duties on children towards parents, which duties are written in the Book of God, as belonging to God.[9]

To have reverence and consideration for one's parents is a matter whose importance is clear to everyone. In all the divinely-inspired books this point has been emphasized; each of the Divine Educators has repeatedly drawn the attention of mankind to it. In the Old Testament, among the many counsels relevant to this topic are these, from the Book of Exodus: 'Honour thy father and thy mother: that thy days may be long upon the land which the Lord thy God giveth thee.' (20:12.) And again, 'And he that smiteth his father, or his mother, shall be surely put to death.' (21:15.) And further, 'And he that curseth his father, or his mother, shall surely be put to death.' (21:17.)

In the Book of Proverbs, we find, 'My son, hear the instruction of thy father, and forsake not the law of thy mother: For they shall be an ornament of grace unto thy head, and chains about thy neck.' (1:8.) And in that same book is recorded the following: 'My son, keep thy father's commandment, and forsake not the law of thy mother: Bind them continually upon thine heart, and tie them about thy neck. When thou goest, it shall lead thee; when thou sleepest, it shall keep thee; and when thou awakest, it shall talk with thee. For the commandment is a lamp; and the law is light.' (6:20.) [1]

In the very first chapter of the Qur'án, God's counsel reads, ' . . . You shall not serve any save God, and to be good to parents . . . ' (2:77.) And in the fourth chapter is written, 'Serve God, and associate naught with Him. Be kind to parents . . . ' (4:40.) And also, in the chapter entitled 'The Night Journey', these words are recorded: 'Thy Lord has decreed you shall not serve any but Him, and to be good to parents, whether one or both of them attains old age with thee; say not to them "Fie" neither chide them, but speak unto them words respectful, and lower to them the wing of humbleness out of mercy and say, "My Lord,

[1] See also Matt. 15:4 and Mark 7:10.

have mercy upon them, as they raised me up when I
was little."' (17:24.)

To strive to honour and show respect to one's
mother and father is an ordinance upheld and emphasized by every religion as well as by civil codes of law.
It has far-reaching moral and humanitarian implications. If the respect, station, and dignity of the
parents are preserved against any encroachment, then
the family – the base on which society rests – will
remain firm and unwavering.

To bring society crashing down to a state of ruin, to
annihilate a nation and drag its inhabitants towards
utter loss can be speedily accomplished by the dis-
integration of family bonds, and the best way to
destroy the family is by dishonouring the parents,
injuring their prestige and transgressing against their
lofty rank. Whoever turns children against their
parents and instils in them a feeling of rebelliousness
towards their mothers and fathers, or, through word
or deed, initiates acts of disobedience and attitudes of
dissension in a family, undoubtedly has as his purpose
the commission of unwholesome and deplorable
actions.

Whoever, on the contrary, assists children to understand the necessity of obedience to and reverence for
parents, thereby encouraging a deep and heart-felt
affection towards the mother and father, affection
which is the foundation of the family's well-being, has
a goal which is rooted in the Scriptures. To teach
respect for parents:

1. From the time the children start talking and
understanding, it is essential that mothers and fathers

alike treat them with the utmost courtesy, taking care not to use harsh words and indecent language. Not for a moment should the parents allow themselves to think that young children are incapable of distinguishing between good and bad, or that they do not care about their personalities; on the contrary, the hearts of children are far more sensitive and delicate than those of grown-ups. They become grief-stricken over the slightest matter.

In everyday conversation with their children, fathers and mothers must take into careful consideration the dignity of their offspring and evaluate every sentence before it is spoken lest the children become hurt or offended by the parents' words. If the children do become hurt, their reaction will be one of suspicion towards the parents, and the feelings of affection which normally exist between parent and child will be effaced. Consideration and respect for the children, on the contrary, enamours them of their parents as well as of their educators, for wise methods used by educators impart the lessons of affection and nobility of character, and do much to strengthen the bonds of friendship.

Many a family has suffered its unity to be utterly demolished from failure to observe this principle, and many a child has, as a result of tongue-lashings and rough treatment, become obstinate and even rebellious towards his parents. It is not improper to mention, in this connection, a sound saying which is common among people in some parts of the world: 'If adults have respect for the young, they safeguard respect for themselves.'

Parents, then, ought always to treat their children considerately and to regard them as intelligent and sensitive human beings. Even if a parent is angry or nervous, an attempt should be made to control himself, to act politely, and not to resort to slander or the use of harsh words. Above all, striking a child should be totally avoided. Coarse treatment of children – even the idea of it – should never be allowed to penetrate the family environment, for it will result in the eradication of courtesy from the characters of the children and cause them to behave rudely towards other members of the family, gradually effacing all traces of love and affection from their hearts. This fact cannot be denied: when parents treat their offspring with respect, their own sense of honour is preserved, and when they do not, the children in turn gradually become disinclined to behave respectfully towards audacious and indiscreet parents.

2. The absolute authority of fathers and mothers in a family must never be misused; care and diligence must be exercised when issuing instructions. If a child is convinced that he is incapable of carrying out a certain task, the parents should not insist on its execution. If instructions are issued which logically and practically cannot be put into effect by the children, it is inevitable that they will not be carried through to completion, and as a result, the station of the parent issuing the orders will be weakened in the sight of the children. When parents insist on difficult things being done, and use harshness and anger as the guarantee, the outcome will be a heightened attitude of rebelliousness in the children.

It is therefore of the utmost importance that parents ponder carefully the consequences of any instructions they may feel inclined to give their children. And this matter should never be neglected by the parents: if a task is truly beyond the child's capacity, then it should not even be mentioned. At the basis of children's resistance and insolence towards their parents is disregard for this principle.

3. From the earliest years children should be raised in the spirit of obedience to their parents. Scriptural verses and the sayings and writings of poets and scholars should be explained to the children. The explanations themselves should be clothed in simple and suitable language, sometimes in the form of counsels, at other times through the use of examples and stories, or even in the language of the learned of both past and present. So important is this matter that fathers and mothers should regard the slightest disobedience to them as a serious form of misbehaviour; even the thought of such a transgression should not occur to the child's mind. If it should happen that a child behaves in a way that is disrespectful to the mother or father, it should immediately be pointed out to him that his action is unwholesome and unbecoming a polite child; that the parents may be offended or saddened, and that, if this happens, it will have distressing consequences for the child concerned, both in this world and in the world to come. The aim should be to caution the child at the time that he commits the actions and utters the words which are disrespectful to the parents.

4. Parents should prevent their offspring from associating with children who disrespect their fathers and mothers and criticize their actions, loudly complaining about them to others. But this should be done with wisdom. Nothing is more lethal to children than

bad friends, and in truth, 'a bad friend has a far worse effect than a bite from a poisonous snake.'

5. It is clear that the mother should never, when in the presence of the children, do or say anything which might lessen their respect for the father, and under no condition should the father belittle the mother in the children's eyes. Rather, these two strong pillars upholding the family should shun every kind of disagreement. In this way, the phoenix of happiness will perch atop their home, and the doors of misfortune and distress will be closed on that household by the Peerless God. So long as the prosperity or adversity of our children is in our own hands, why should we not tread the path indicated by the Prophets? And why should we undermine the future happiness of our offspring through negligence?

9

A WELL-TRAINED MIND

The heart of 'Abdu'l-Bahá longeth, in its love, to find that Bahá'í young people, each and all, are known throughout the world for their intellectual attainments.[1]

Strive as much as possible to become proficient . . . for in accordance with the divine teachings the acquisition of sciences and the perfection of arts are considered acts of worship.[2]

MAN POSSESSES PHYSICAL and intellectual powers. The five physical faculties perceive material objects, while the intellectual powers are able to perceive truths and realities. The combination of these two powers confers the mantle of humanity on mankind, enabling and preparing him to attain the highest degrees of material and spiritual civilization.

The intellectual, or inner, powers can be divided into five faculties:

1. *The common faculty*, which is the intermediary between the five physical senses and the inner powers; it conveys whatever the physical senses discern to the inner powers.

2. *The power of the imagination*, which conceives and forms images of things.

3. *The power of thought*, which reflects on the realities of things.

4. *The power of comprehension*, which comprehends the reality of things.

5. *The power of memory*, which retains and stores whatever a person imagines, thinks, and comprehends.

The development of the mental faculties is an involved and abstruse subject in the field of psychology. Experts in the field have written hundreds of books and articles defining and explaining this matter, but they are not easy for those untrained in the science of education to understand. Nevertheless, at least a cursory look at this important question is essential to fathers and mothers. The present writer, according to his own understanding and knowledge, will briefly outline the subject, but he requests that readers ponder its significance and not satisfy themselves with one superficial reading.

Perception and Recognition

There are certain pillars which have been established as the unshakeable supports of the Faith of God. The mightiest of these is learning and the use of the mind, the expansion of consciousness, and insight into the realities of the universe and the hidden mysteries of Almighty God.[3]

Many scholars have stated that the acts of 'recognizing' and 'perceiving' are natural functions of the human mind and lead to comprehension, imagination, thoughts, and ideas.

There is a basic difference between 'perception' and 'feeling'. When a person feels something, that thing – directly and without any intermediary – elicits a response from his nervous system, as, for example, when feelings of heat, cold, hunger, thirst, and the like are experienced. At this time the inner self seems to be in an inactive state.

But if a person wants to differentiate, through perception, between one thing and another, then the mental faculties are immediately brought into play. The power and activity of the human mind become apparent, for perception and recognition primarily consist in differentiating and distinguishing. When someone says, 'I am familiar with that book,' or 'I know this person,' he means that he has no problem in differentiating between that book and others, or that he can easily distinguish this person from other people.

The mind's activity is apparent not only with respect to the material world, but also in the world of abstraction, the non-material world: the human mind differentiates between ideas too.

Besides this, the mental faculties perform another significant task in establishing and classifying the common properties of things that resemble each other. It is in this way that categories can be established and sciences in their specific and real sense can be introduced. When, for example, someone asks himself, 'What is this object?' he immediately perceives how that object resembles certain others. For instance, he deduces that 'the new object belongs to a group of things which are called 'trees', since from every aspect it resembles trees.' After perceiving this, he rapidly judges that 'this object must be a tree too.'

Perception and recognition, therefore, consist in this: on the one hand, an individual perceives the relationship that exists between various objects, linking and categorizing them, and on the other hand, he comprehends the distinctive features of an object. To be more precise, he identifies that specific thing and does not confuse it with others, so that at any given moment he can indicate that 'this object is a book,' 'that is an ink-pot,' 'this is a pen,' and 'that is a piece of writing paper'.

A mind that is innately superior and vigorous, and that has been properly developed through discipline and study, is able to discover hitherto unknown phenomena and cause the different sciences to yield up their secrets. And the vastly superior human mind, which has been manifested throughout the world in people of genius, is able to perceive unusual or concealed connections that exist between things and that, because of their minute nature, are not readily perceived by people of normal intelligence. As a result, this type of mind is capable of discovering the secrets of the world.

Memory

All blessings are divine in origin but none can be compared with this power of intellectual investigation and research which is an eternal gift producing fruits of unending delight . . . Briefly; it is an eternal blessing and divine bestowal, the supreme gift of God to man. Therefore you should put forward your most earnest efforts towards the acquisition of science and arts. The greater your attainment, the higher your standard in the divine purpose.[4]

The outstanding progress in the advancement of science over the ages is due in no small measure to the part which memory plays and the influence it exerts on every phase of mental activity. By whatever means impressions of the outside world penetrated the inner powers of man, whatever perception led him to deduce, and whatever effect his environment produced on him – all would immediately fade away but for the power of retaining impressions of past experience. If man were deprived of this faculty, nothing could be perceived or comprehended, and mental activity and intelligence would be fruitless and come to nothing.

For instance, if we meet someone but do not record his face and features in our memories, as soon as he disappears from our sight no recognition or association between us and that person remains. By the same token, if we had no memory, nothing we had seen or observed in the past would have any meaning, and our powers of perception would be limited to the present, and confined to vibrations of the nervous system which occur when feelings and impressions are experienced. For example, if someone devoid of memory were to hear a melodious song, then despite its interception by the sense of hearing, that song could not be implanted in the mind, and as soon as it ceased, no trace of it would remain with the listener.

Without the faculty of memory, therefore, nothing perceived by the outer senses could leave an impression on the mind, and as soon as the material things creating the stimuli were removed, it would be as though they had never existed. In such circumstances, the relationships between the realities of created things would remain undiscovered, and man would find himself powerless to unravel the mysteries of nature.

For this reason, psychologists have acknowledged the great importance of the power of memory, and described methods of strengthening it.

How the Memory Works

The memory has the capacity to mentally retain impressions of past experience, and recollect them and distinguish between them as required. Recollection does not concern itself only with thoughts, but with all conditions of the self and with all mental states. Whatever the intelligence discerns and whatever finds its way to the mind – be it through feeling or perception – will be preserved in the memory and recollected at appropriate times.

Memory has two aspects: personal and general. The one records and registers each person's history, whether important or trivial, and makes him aware at any given moment of his past and present states, while the other connects an individual with other people and with the world at large, assisting him to recognize his own self and his traits, and acquainting him with the different things, persons, incidents, and events around him. The memory thus serves as a means of connecting human beings with the outside world – the bond that holds society together – and is the cause of relating the past to the present and future.

The memory, in general, has four duties:

A. *to retain thoughts*
B. *to recall what has been retained*
C. *to distinguish between the different things stored in its repository*
D. *to specify the time of the occurrences that have been recorded*

That is to say, whatever is perceived leaves an impression on the memory and is retained; that same impression is recalled at the appropriate time; each thing remembered is distinguishable from other feelings and perceptions; and the time when an impression entered the mind is clearly indicated.

The memory, therefore, in everything that is remembered and recollected, performs a four-fold duty. These four stages will be briefly explained.

A. Retention of thoughts

To try to understand the process of thought-retention is an arduous and involved task, and in order to put the subject into perspective, psychologists have found themselves compelled to resort to the use of analogies. Some have likened the memory to a storehouse in which thoughts, after entering the mind, are stored and concealed, to be later recalled under specific conditions. Others have compared it to layers of sand on which lines are drawn. A few have described the memory as being similar to a camera able to take an infinity of images. And still others have indicated that the faculty of memory can be compared to a tape-recorder capable of repeating whatever it recorded.

Some experts hold the opinion that whatever affects our inner selves, whether through actions, reactions or something perceived, leaves an impression. The retention of impressions is, therefore, one of the characteristics of the human mind. Impressions are formed and retention takes place under specific conditions. One is the *physical condition*, or physiology, of the person concerned. For thought-retention to function normally, sound physical health must be maintained and the nervous system must remain unimpaired. Anything which might prove injurious to health should be avoided, since physical well-being has a direct relationship with the functioning of the memory, and an individual suffering from illness is naturally deprived of a strong memory. Those who wish to cultivate a well-trained memory should take steps to protect their health (widely-distributed scientific publications are available on this subject). This calls for abstinence from alcoholic beverages, avoidance of smoking, of breathing polluted and contaminated air, of prolonged sleeplessness, of lechery, and of overeating (which leads to digestive disorders).

For a strong impression to be made on the memory and a high degree of retention assured, certain *psychological conditions* are necessary:

1. *Intensity of impression.* The more intense the impression made at the time of perception, the longer will it endure in the memory. Almost everybody has experienced things which, because of the strong impressions they made, have never been effaced from the memory. If we liken the memory to a camera, then the sharpness of the impression will largely depend upon a strong enough source of light so as to effect an image on the film. It is clear, therefore, that the more intense the effect produced by an incident and the stronger the resultant impression, the deeper will be the impression left on the memory, and the longer will be its duration.

2. *Degree of excitement.* Besides intensity of impression, the degree of excitement produced by an incident plays an almost equally significant role in the process of retention. The greater the excitement or agitation caused by an occurrence, the longer will be the duration of the impression in the memory. Any event which generates joy and happiness, or produces anxiety and distress, will be retained in the memory

longer than events which do not produce these feelings. If we compare the memory to a vast sea, then
agitation and excitement are produced by the wind;
the harder it blows, the higher and deeper will be the
crests and hollows of the waves.

3. *Level of concentration.* Concentration has a profound influence on memory, for the more attention a
person gives to some particular matter, the longer will
it be remembered. Some people are able to memorize
things quickly, but forget them easily, while others
painstakingly commit something to memory, but retain
it well. It is, of course, easier to make markings on
mounds of sand than to engrave them on marble, but
whatever is engraved on marble will endure for ages,
while lines drawn on sand will be rapidly effaced by the
wind and waves.

Concentration also serves as the perfect assistant to
the memory, for it clarifies what is to be remembered.
Anything which is vague, or devoid of definite and
clear-cut meaning, makes its way into the memory
with immense difficulty, and then is easily forgotten.
But whatever is clear and well understood is registered
easily, and is retained in the memory for a long period
of time.

When all the senses are alert and the attention is
concentrated, it is as though the rays of the sun are
passing through a magnifying glass, whereas absent-
mindedness and a short attention span are like these
same rays passing through ordinary glass: when light
from the sun is refracted by the magnifier, the intensity
of its heat is greater than the temperature required to
light a fire, but when this same light passes through
ordinary glass, it will be diffused, and produce no

noticeable heat. By the same token, the rôle of concentration and alertness is of the utmost importance in the development of a strong memory.

4. *Discipline and order*. The power of memory will be more evident, our thoughts will be clearer and more distinct, and sound mental relationships will be better established if the relationship of discipline and order to the memory process is acknowledged. Poetry, for this reason, is memorized more easily than prose, and if prose is orderly and logical, it will be better remembered than writing which is incoherent and rambling.

5. *Repetition* is more important than anything else for memory work, and most people are able to memorize and retain very little without its use. It often happens that we memorize certain matters simply by being repeatedly subjected to them, in spite of our lack of desire or interest in learning them. For this reason, some experts have come to regard the memory process and repetition work as inseparable.

B. Recollection of thoughts

Thought-recall can be voluntary or involuntary. That is, it takes place either spontaneously, or as a result of volition, as demonstrated by the common expressions, 'such and such occurred to me,' and 'I recollect such and such a subject.' In the first instance, an involuntary action is being referred to, while in the second, the speaker is indicating a voluntary action.

Thoughts long stored in the recesses of the memory often enter the consciousness on their own. For example, an individual may be occupied with some task and his thoughts and senses duly concentrated on the matter at hand, when strains of music which he has heard long before suddenly pop into his mind, and he finds himself humming the tune. Perhaps this will happen again and again during the same day, for even though the person does not want it to, the music clings to his mind and senses, and disrupts his current thinking; he may even confess his powerlessness to prevent it from doing so.

Thoughts and ideas which leave a strong impression on the memory are recalled with comparable intensity, and often a conflict between present impressions and past memory arises. Whenever something triggers past memories, they immediately occupy our thought channels to the extent that no room for current feelings and impressions remains.

C. Discernment

Discernment is another important function of the memory. When a person wishes to distinguish one thought from others in his mind, he should have no trouble in recognizing that that thought was stored in his memory at some particular time in the past. For this reason, discernment cannot be disassociated from the time factor. In addition, the person should be fully aware at the time that the thought is distinct from his present perceptions and feelings, and also that it has not sprung from his imagination. If the act of discernment occurs in this manner, there can be no doubt that thought recall has taken place.

When, for instance, someone sees another person or hears a song, he should be able to discern accurately that he has definitely seen that person or heard that song before, and that whatever he is seeing or hearing now is precisely the same as it was when stored in his memory. There is then no doubt that the previous impression is now being recalled.

There is a significant difference between thought-recall and current perception:

1. Perception is far more intense and much clearer than recollection. In the opinion of Herbert Spencer, the perception of things is a strong factor, while thought-recollection is a weak factor. If someone visits the cathedral of Notre-Dame, observes its features, and after some days pauses to reconsider his visit, he finds that he is unable to recall clearly all its details, leaving no doubt that his memories of the building are weaker and more vague than his original perception of it.

2. Perception occurs involuntarily, and enters the intelligence forcibly. When a person is standing in front of the cathedral of Notre-Dame and his eyes are open, he cannot help seeing it. But his recollection of the scene, on the other hand, comes about as a result of his own volition, and this impression can fade from his memory or be altered.

3. When a person sees something, previous impressions affect its relevancy. For instance, when I see my desk, thoughts of the library, its essential books, and my whole study come to mind while perceiving it. Current perceptions, however, often render the recollection vague. For example, when I recall a desk which I saw at a merchant's home, at the same time I visualize my own desk which is in my library. The intensity of the latter impression, namely, the visualizing of my own desk, changes the mental image of the merchant's desk into a weak recollection.

D. *The time factor*

Specifying the time of what was perceived – the last stage of recollection – consists in allotting a definite time for each distinct impression which has been recalled. That is to say, when the stage of discernment is complete, and the place at which the impression occurred has been established, the specific time of its occurrence should also be considered in order that every aspect of the impression may become clear.

For example, I recollect having travelled to a certain city, and I am positive that this trip did take place, but with the passage of time the journey has become clouded in my mind, and I cannot put my finger on the exact time of year in which it took place. In order to pin down the date of its occurrence, in my mind I travel from the present into the distant past and start searching through my memory, reviewing link by link the chain of events related to this particular undertaking. During this inquisition, one thing which comes to mind is that during the trip, I had entered a guesthouse in which a very beautiful wood stove was burning, and I had asked the waiter to provide me with more dry wood, because I was enjoying the warmth. Immediately, I realize that my trip took place in winter. At this point, the time element has been solved, and my inner search comes to a halt.

If the mutual dealings between the self and the intelligence took place in an orderly and well-defined manner, then the task of linking an event with the time of its occurrence would be very easy. We would simply trace the string of events recorded in our memories until arriving at the exact impression we were seeking. But it is not as easy as all that, for some of our impressions and experiences have become so obscured that their recollection in the mind is well-nigh impossible – hence, the observation that one of the aspects of memory is forgetfulness.

For whatever remains firm in our memories, however, the last stage of recollection is complete when its time factor has been established.

Diseases of the Memory

We have already seen that the memory is composed of various elements, each with distinct characteristics. These elements sometimes become afflicted with sicknesses and disorders.

In general, diseases of the memory can be divided into two categories:

A. loss of memory
B. extraordinary intensity of memory

The most common disease which afflicts the memory is amnesia; it can weaken the power of recall to such a degree that all recollection of the past is lost.

A. Amnesia manifests itself in different ways:

1. *General amnesia.* This condition may last for only a few minutes, or persist for a number of years, during which time the person so afflicted remembers nothing from his past. A fall, a blow to the head, or an acute fever such as that caused by typhoid (even though it may be of brief duration), can reduce to nothing all the knowledge that the person has acquired throughout his life. Occasionally, general amnesia manifests itself intermittently and at fixed intervals in a person. This is

called temporary amnesia, or temporary loss of memory.

2. *Gradual amnesia.* The person so afflicted first loses contact with what has been most recently learned, and then little by little forgets about his past. This affliction can continue until finally all knowledge of the childhood years is also forgotten.

3. *Partial amnesia.* In this case, the afflicted person cannot recollect some things, but retains the power to recall others. For instance, he may totally forget his knowledge of mathematics and music, but other facets of learning will remain unimpaired. This type of amnesia can take so many forms that it is not possible to list them all. For example, some people suffering from this disease may forget their own names, others may lose track of colours and numbers, and still others may forget how to use parts of speech, such as verbs and conjunctions.

B. The second disease mentioned above concerns the experiencing of extraordinarily intense thought-recall. When this happens in extreme cases, everything deposited in the memory seems suddenly to manifest itself at incredible speed. Such a condition has been experienced by many people who have recovered from a near bout with death, and, on returning to a normal state, have described how they saw their past life before them as though depicted on a movie screen.

When this affliction only partially manifests itself in an individual, he remembers things which had been so completely forgotten that not even the smallest fraction of his attention had been given to them. For instance, he may experience this condition during a severe fever, at which time he remembers and utters thoughts which, under normal conditions, neither he himself nor others would believe possible.

Different Kinds of Memory

Psychologists, through the study of aberrations of the memory, have established that there are different kinds of memory, and that not everyone possesses the same type of retentive power. Some reasons for this are hereditary differences, specific susceptibilities, superior development of some of the senses, and different habits. These, and other factors, give everyone a different kind of memory, and in this sense, differentiate the individual members of society from each other.

Basically, memory functions in two areas: *the external memory*, which pertains to the senses, and is concerned with things; and *the mental or intellectual memory*, which pertains to abstractions and thoughts.

The kinds of memory which pertain to the senses are:

A. *visual memory*
B. *auditory memory*
C. *action memory*

Each of these has differences of degree as well: for instance, in the area of visual memory, artists, sculptors and engineers have a gift for remembering colour combinations, shapes and forms, and spatial relations. As to auditory memory, musicians are better trained than most others in this area, and as a result they are able to commit to memory lengthy musical scores. And as for action memory, it is well known that people who are blind are usually better able than others to distinguish mentally between the tactile qualities of things.

The kinds of memory which pertain to abstractions and thoughts have differences of degree as well. For instance, the retentive abilities of mathematicians, philosophers and naturalists differ.

From this, it can be seen that people, from a comparison of their memories, fall into different categories: for one person, the visual memory is stronger; for another, auditory memory is better trained; while for someone else, mental retention resulting from actions is superior. That is, one person has greater retentive powers with matters which are introduced into the memory through the visual sense, a different person remembers things better which he learns through the use of the sense of hearing, while another person finds that he is better able to recall impressions that have been acquired through muscular movements involving writing, reading aloud, or touching.

We must recognize, however, that none of these forms of memory exist independently in their pure form, but that all are combined and function together in human beings. For different people, however, these factors which affect the memory vary in intensity, so that one factor may strongly influence the memory of one person, while exerting a weaker influence on that of another. The distinct characteristics of each person's principal retentive faculty result from the degree of intensity of these different factors.

What is a Good Memory?

Just as people's memories differ innately in kind, they are also different in degree: a memory can be well-trained or defective. The characteristics of a good memory are as follows:

1. Material is easily grasped, and is rapidly transferred to the retentive faculty. This can happen in such a way that a person, after repeating a matter only once, is able to comprehend it and store it in his memory.

2. Whatever is committed to memory remains fast and firm. That is, whatever is memorized remains firmly rooted in the memory, and is easily recalled when necessary; when a person wishes to recollect a certain matter, no great effort is required, and he is always ready with an answer.

These two factors constitute the distinguishing features of a good memory, enabling the person who possesses them to learn things easily, remember them for long periods of time, and recall them at will. Whoever does not possess these characteristics has a defective memory.

Training and Developing the Memory

For a great many years the question of whether it was possible to train and strengthen the memory was a topic of discussion among psychologists. Eventually they agreed that, even though the memory is a natural adjunct of the human mind and to alter its essential make-up is not possible, the observation of certain guide-lines of sound mental and physical hygiene will help to train and strengthen the memory. No one, therefore, should regard his memory as a hopeless case, or neglect the development of this divine bestowal. Rather, every member of the human race ought to take steps continually to foster the development of the memory and, by following a few guidelines, attempt to rectify its apparent shortcomings and increase its power of retention and recall.

There are many recommendations for strengthening the memory, the essence of which are as follows:

1. Inasmuch as good bodily health has a strong bearing on the proper functioning of the memory, every physical problem should be promptly dealt with and rectified, whether it is a problem of the nervous system, the digestive system, or any other physical function. The following conditions enhance the functioning of the memory: the presence of clean and pure air at the time of mental activity, the elimination of near-sightedness and impaired hearing, the curing of tonsillitis, the observation of sound principles of hygiene in eating, relaxed and undisturbed sleep, exercise in fresh air, and the avoidance of narcotics and alcohol.

2. The place of study should be sufficiently quiet and adequately lit so that the attention can be concentrated on learning; the result will be a higher degree of comprehension and retention.

3. While reading, writing, and studying, try to concentrate and focus the thoughts on the work at hand.

4. After a chapter of a book has been read, write a summary of it; this helps one understand it.

5. Before reading, writing or memorizing anything, establish the objective of the undertaking; in this way,

the mental faculties can be concentrated on the goal. For instance, if the main purpose of reading something is to commit it to memory, then questions about the meaning of specific details should be held in abeyance. And if the objective is to arrive at an overall understanding, then do not give too much attention to single words and phrases.

6. Stop work as soon as you feel the first signs of fatigue.

7. If the material to be memorized is extensive, it should be worked on over a period of days, so that no unnecessary pressure is brought to bear.

8. When something has to be memorized, read the passage in its entirety instead of dividing it into sections, and repeat it several times.

9. Carefully evaluate which kind of memory you have and then rely on that when you wish to memorize something. If, for instance, you have a highly-developed visual memory, then try to learn things visually; if you possess a well-trained auditory memory, then rely more on your sense of hearing; and if your memory functions better by doing, then you can probably memorize passages easiest by writing and rewriting them.

10. The very first reading of a passage to be memorized should be carried out with care, for if a mistake is made at this time and permeates to the memory, the task of correcting it will prove to be extremely difficult.

11. There should be a relationship, whether through the words or their meanings, between the different parts of the material to be memorized, so that it is better retained.

12. The principal method of committing things to

memory is through repetition. The more often the material to be memorized is repeated, the better will it be learned. Of course, this must be coupled with comprehension and concentrated attention.

These points, if observed, will greatly assist in strengthening the retentive faculty, and in developing the mind. Of course, the psychological conditions referred to earlier should not be disregarded.

Knowledge of Science is Helpful

Give them the advantage of every useful kind of knowledge. [5]

Although to acquire the sciences and arts is the greatest glory of mankind, this is so only on condition that man's river flow into the mighty Sea, and draw from God's ancient source His inspiration. [6]

Psychologists are of the opinion that parents who are unfamiliar with simple scientific subjects will be unable to answer their children's questions satisfactorily. A sample follows of some scientific topics about which parents, if need be, can obtain more information from public libraries. These matters can be explained to children as the opportunities arise. In this way, parents will increase the knowledge of their children, and rear them in the spirit of learning. Here then, in relatively simple language, are some samples of the type of scientific information which parents may find useful for answering their children's questions.

A. The Earth

1. The earth is a spherical substance, shaped like an orange or a watermelon. Three-quarters of it is covered with water, and the rest is dry land.

2. The earth both rotates on its axis and travels around the sun, and these two kinds of movement take place at the same time – something like a toy top, which spins while at the same time tracing large circles on the floor.

3. The rotation of the earth around its axis, which completes one full turn every twenty-four hours, gives us days and nights. The movement of the earth around the sun, which requires 365 days, 6 hours, 9 minutes and 9 seconds for one complete revolution, is the cause of the different seasons.

4. Just as a magnet draws a metal needle towards itself, so does the earth attract objects towards itself. For this reason, we stay on the ground, and are not tossed about.

5. Even though the earth moves at great speed, we do not feel its movement, just as passengers on a ship are unaware of the movement of the ship.

6. All liquid substances are spherical, unless they strike a barrier and change shape. Raindrops and hailstones are spherical as they fall towards the ground. The sun, the moon, and the stars are also spherical. Our earth cooled through the liquid state to naturally become spherical.

7. There are many proofs that the earth is round, and we will point out some of them:

a. When a ship is nearing a port, someone watching its approach from the sea-side notices the upper part of the vessel first, and then, little by little, the rest of it becomes visible.

b. Likewise, when a ship is departing, to an observer on shore the main part of the ship disappears from vision before the mast does. If the earth were not spherical, the ship could still be seen through strong binoculars however far it travelled. To the naked eye, the mast would disappear from sight more rapidly than the body of the ship, since the ship itself, being far larger than the mast, should naturally be more visible from a distance.

c. When a ship is approaching shore, its passengers first see the tops of the highest buildings in the city they are going towards, and the smaller buildings become visible later.

d. When the sun sets and disappears from sight, if someone is carried up in a balloon, he will see the sun again. When the sun disappears from view a second time, he can see it once again by going still higher.

e. If a traveller approaches a city located on a vast plain, the first things he sees are the tallest structures, and then, the whole city gradually appears before him.

f. When the earth comes directly between the sun and the moon, causing an eclipse of the moon, the shadow of the earth which can be seen on the moon is spherical.

8. The earth is 1,300,000 times smaller than the sun, and 50 times larger than the moon.

9. If a person travels 65 miles in 24 hours and continues his journey at the same rate and in the same direction for 365 days, he will have gone completely around the earth and returned to the same spot from which he had departed.

B. Celestial Bodies

The celestial bodies are divided into three main

groups:
1. fixed stars
2. planets
3. comets

1. The fixed stars produce their own light, and do not receive their brightness from other sources. Their distance from each other always appears to be the same. If we look at the sky on a clear night, without the assistance of any viewing instruments, we will see about 6,000 stars. But with the help of telescopes, thousands and millions of stars can be seen, to a number which defies calculation.

2. Planets do not produce their own light, but receive their brightness from the sun. Since the light they receive becomes noticeable to us at night, we can easily see some of these planets. In the same way that a mirror facing the sun reflects sunlight in the opposite direction, so the planets reflect the light they receive from the sun, and we can see these other planets from the earth. The planets turn on their axes at different speeds, and also travel around the sun.

The names of the planets in our solar system are Mercury, Venus, Earth, Mars, Jupiter, Saturn, Uranus, Neptune and Pluto. In addition to these planets, hundreds of planetoids have been discovered by astronomers.

Most of the planets have one or more natural satellites which revolve around them, and these are called moons. Mars, for instance, has two; Jupiter, thirteen; Saturn, eight; Uranus, four; Neptune, one; and the Earth, one.

3. Comets are like planets in that they do not gener-

ate light, but receive it from the sun. Comets look like a gaseous cloud, and have a brightly-lit head and a faintly-lit tail. They can be seen from time to time in the night sky as they come from outer space to travel around the sun and then return spacewards again.

C. Sunrise and Sunset

1. The sun is a spherical body, and gives off tremendous light and heat. Even though it may appear to us that the sun rises in the East each morning, crosses the sky, and sets in the West, this is not so; it is the earth's rotation which creates this illusion. In the same way, when a ship slowly moves away from shore, it seems to the passengers as though the harbour is travelling away from them.

2. Every twenty-five and a half days, the sun rotates once on its axis. In that part of the earth which faces the sun, it is day-time, while in the other part, it is night. For this reason, when it is day-time in Asia and Europe, it is night-time in the continents of North and South America. And when Americans get up in the morning to go to work, Asians and Europeans are preparing to go to sleep.

3. When the sun appears on the horizon, we say that it has risen, and that point is called East. When the sun sinks below the horizon, we say that it has set, and that point is called West. In actual fact, of course, the sun neither rises nor sets, nor does it have an East or a West. Since the earth makes one complete turn on its axis in a West to East direction once in every 24 hours, it only appears to us that the sun rises in the East and sets in the West.

4. The distance between the earth and the sun is about 93 million miles, and it takes 8 minutes for light from the sun to reach the earth.

D. *The Moon*

1. The moon is also a spherical body, and a natural satellite of the earth. It receives its brightness from the sun, and noticeably lights up that part of the earth which is experiencing night. Even though the moon is far smaller than the planets, it appears to us to be much larger because it is so much closer to the earth than the other heavenly bodies.

2. According to scientific studies which have been carried out, no water, air, or living creatures have been found on the moon, whose surface is rocky and pitted with craters.

3. It takes 27 days, 7 hours, and 43 minutes for the moon to make one complete revolution around the earth. It travels around the sun, together with the earth, once a year.

4. As the moon revolves around the earth and rotates on its own axis, we see its different 'phases', and the 'lunar months', recorded by some types of calendars, are measured in this way. Sometimes we cannot see the moon at all, because its dark side is towards us. Then it appears in the form of a crescent, followed by the phases: first quarter, full moon, last quarter; finally, only a very small portion of it is visible, and then it disappears from sight altogether. When that part of the moon which receives light from the sun does not face the earth, naturally we will not see it. If a narrow strip of the part receiving sunlight faces us, we see it in the form of a crescent, and when

the entire part which receives light faces us, this phase is called a full moon.

5. The eclipses of the moon and sun which sometimes occur are also due to the movement of the moon, for when the earth is directly between the sun and the moon, light from the sun is not able to reach the moon. This always coincides with a full moon. When the moon comes directly between the earth and the sun and prevents sunlight from striking much of the earth, this is called an eclipse of the sun. In places where the moon completely prevents the light of the sun from reaching the earth, it is called a total eclipse of the sun, and in places where some of the sun's light reaches the earth, it is called a partial eclipse of the sun. And also, if the earth completely prevents sunlight from striking the face of the moon, it is called a total eclipse of the moon, and if it prevents only a part of the sunlight from reaching the moon, it is called a partial eclipse of the moon.

E. Air and Atmosphere

1. Air is a light substance which is clear and pure. Because of the extreme minuteness of the particles which compose air, it cannot be seen by the naked eye – except when layers of air are seen together, in which case it appears to be blue. For this reason, we do not see the air which surrounds us, such as the air in a room, but when we gaze at the sky, we see it as a blue dome. This dome consists of layers of air one on top of the other.

2. Air is essential for most forms of life, including human beings. Just like a watermelon skin which surrounds the edible part of the fruit, air surrounds the

globe to a thickness of 110,000 metres.

3. Clouds, fog, rain, snow, hail, wind, thunder, and lightning are all formed in the air.

Clouds. The warmth of the sun causes some of the water in the oceans, seas, lakes, and rivers to evaporate. Since this vapour is lighter than air, it rises to a certain level, where it accumulates and forms clouds. Clouds, therefore, result from the accumulation and compression of water vapour in the air.

Fog. The heat of the sun often causes heavy mists to form over bodies of water. If the weather is not very warm, the mist will stay close to the surface of the water, and as the temperature rises, so will the mist. This thick vapour which does not rise above the layers of air is called fog.

Rain. Condensed vapour, which forms in clouds, becomes water-drops and falls to the ground from above the air layers. These water-drops are called rain.

Snow and Hail. If the condensed vapour forming in clouds comes into contact with cold layers of air, it freezes, and the frozen drops fall to the ground in the form of snow and hail.

The Wind. Since air accumulates layer over layer, a temperature difference between these layers causes them to move, creating wind. If this motion is slight, we feel it as a light breeze; if the movement of the air is intense, and there is a lot of wind, then we experience a storm.

Thunder and Lightning. When two layers of clouds move near each other, static electricity is transferred, and the clouds become charged with this power. When two clouds, one with a positive charge of electricity and one with a negative charge, pass near each other, a discharge of electricity occurs between them. This is seen as lightning, and when it disturbs the air, thunder is created. When lightning discharges between a cloud and the earth, it can split and burn trees, and is capable of destroying buildings.

In order to prevent damage from lightning, Benjamin Franklin, the famous American scientist, instructed that a well should be dug near all tall structures, in a suitable place, and that a tall column should be built from the well; to the top of this column is attached an iron bar whose tip is coated with platinum. A long chain runs down the column with one end fastened to the bar, and the other end submerged in the water at the bottom of the well. When lightning occurs in that area, it will naturally strike the top of this instrument, since it is taller than all the buildings in the vicinity, and the electrical charge will be carried to the bottom of the well, where it will be neutralized in the ground. If the buildings are located near seas, lakes, rivers, or pools, there is no need to dig a well. This invention has been greatly refined, and now lightning rods are easily provided. Their use has saved many buildings from partial or total destruction.

It is clear that the human mind penetrates and influences all matters, whether physical or intellectual. Educators, therefore, should fully understand its importance and may bear the following points in mind so as to be able to train this extraordinary faculty in children.

1. Education does *not* consist in giving children as many lessons as possible, teaching them a multitude of diverse subjects, or cramming their mental faculties

with every sort of information. On the contrary, the objective of a good teacher should be to help the child understand essential matters as far as possible, to discover the scope of his pupil's knowledge and, through the use of principles of psychology, develop it.

2. Any teacher who, by burdening a pupil's memory, tries to increase the child's knowledge in a short time, has failed to recognize the nature of his responsibility, and shows no interest whatever in his student's future.

3. The amount and range of acquired knowledge is not as important as the quality of that knowledge and the method of imparting it to the pupil. For, in acquiring essential learning, a taste for thinking and diligence should be generated within the child, as well as an eagerness to discover and understand the phenomena of the world of creation.

4. A devoted teacher is one who not only creates in his students an interest in perceiving truth and acquiring knowledge, but simultaneously teaches them proper conduct, trustworthiness, faithfulness, and other praiseworthy characteristics. In this way, deposited in each child will be a treasure which can be gradually drawn on to ensure his continued development.

5. Real education consists in establishing a firm and carefully-laid foundation for learning in young children, and not in straining and tiring their mental faculties.

Parents must not for a moment think that the more the retentive faculties of their children are burdened at school and the more their brains stuffed with various subjects, the better they are doing in their studies.

Rather, they should be aware that the human mind has a specific capacity at every stage of its development, and if it is overburdened by unbearably difficult tasks, there will be detrimental consequences. For this reason, parents should direct their attention more towards the quality of their children's studies than towards their quantity.

MORAL AND SOCIAL TRAINING

*In a time to come, morals will degenerate to an extreme
degree. It is essential that children be reared in the
Bahá'í way, that they may find happiness both in this
world and the next. If not, they shall be beset by sorrows
and troubles, for human happiness is founded upon
spiritual behaviour.*[1]

MANY PEOPLE, in thinking about the plight of humanity today, may consider the time when 'morals will
degenerate to an extreme degree' to be already upon
us. Against this background of widespread corruption
and general lack of confidence, children somehow
have to be educated to a high moral standard. Shoghi
Effendi wrote: 'These Bahá'í children are of such great
importance to the future. They will live in times, and
have to meet problems, which never faced their elders.
And the Cause alone can equip them to properly serve
the needs of a future, war-weary, disillusioned, unhappy humanity. So their task will be very great and a
very responsible one, and too much care cannot be
devoted to their upbringing and preparation.'[2]

Obedience

*The law must reign and not the individual; thus will the
world become a place of beauty and true brotherhood
will be realized.*[3]

The habit of obedience is one of the characteristics which children should learn.

Observing divinely-ordained religious laws, and complying with the rules laid down by a just government constitute the foundation of the material and spiritual well-being of a nation. Every country will flourish and prosper whose citizens see submission to laws enacted by those in authority as the standard for their actions. For example, in certain countries, the following regulations are enforced: in theatres, buses, and trains as well as in many public buildings, smoking is prohibited; motorists are obliged to observe specific speed limits; pedestrians must follow certain rules; polluting lakes and streams, and throwing rubbish on roads, are unlawful acts.

If the citizens of these countries observe these and similar rules and regulations, and diligently carry out their social responsibilities, then their welfare and tranquillity will be definitely assured. But if, out of self-interest, a number of individuals are unconcerned with the lot of the masses and ignore most laws and regulations – committing any act that their hearts may devise, and regarding the breaking of laws as an act of courage – then chaos and anarchy will reign in that country, causing disturbances to the majority of its people, eradicating all thoughts of peace and tranquillity, and eventually disillusioning a weary and destitute population, while the machinery of society grinds to a halt.

In order that children may acquire this noble attitude of obedience, the parents must adhere to certain points. The same methods apply here as in teaching respect for parents.

1. Mothers and fathers should attempt to foster the spirit of obedience in their children from the earliest years. In kind and compassionate language, they should strive to inculcate the concepts that reverence and consideration for parents are obligatory and essential, that respect for elders has been divinely-ordained, and that a child who does not obey his parents will be accounted responsible in the sight of God, and ridiculed by society.

2. Whenever the parents wish to assign a task to a child, they should first carefully consider the nature of the work involved and avoid requests which are beyond the capacity of children and which might lead to disobedience and rebelliousness.

3. In schools, the teachers should take every opportunity to impress upon their students the necessity of obedience to fathers and mothers and to the teachers themselves. Through the use of examples, an instructor can explain the benefits of obedience and the detrimental effects of disobedience. For instance, he can explain that if the various parts of the human body such as the hands, feet, eyes, and ears do not carry out the directives of the mind, but shirk its commands, then a state of chaos will prevail within the 'domain' of the body, and any semblance of unity between mind and body will be next to non-existent. Likewise, if the members of a family do not obey the father and mother, and if everyone acts according to his own desires, will that family function properly? And if the dwellers of a city ignore the regulations established by the government, and if each person does as he pleases – without any consideration whatsoever for the public good – will that city have any peace or

tranquillity? In short, the indispensability of obedience should, through every means, be realized and appreciated by children, so that they do not permit themselves to become headstrong and obstinate.

4. Social institutions, too, can promote these interests through films, plays, newspaper and magazine articles, books, and the like. If this attitude is established, strengthened and continually reinforced in all members of society, then complete harmony will prevail, and a multitude of deplorable wrongdoings will be prevented.

The importance of this subject from the view-point of religion is equally clear, for one of the meanings of faith is 'implicit obedience'. When people recognize and, through perception, reasoning, and proofs, acknowledge their belief in a Manifestation of God, and regard His teachings and laws as the only sure source of guidance for mankind, then they must certainly obey His precepts, and not permit themselves to deviate in the slightest from His commandments.

It can be readily acknowledged that obedience in all these matters constitutes the best hope for the felicity and well-being of mankind. Parents, educators, instructors, those vested with authority, and all others who are engaged in promoting the physical, intellectual and spiritual betterment of the human race should give this indispensable matter their complete attention, and assist with the establishment of this praiseworthy quality.

Discipline and Order

Discipline of some sort, whether physical, moral or intellectual, is indeed indispensable, and no training can be said to be complete and fruitful if it disregards this element.[4]

A child that is cleanly, agreeable, of good character, well-behaved – even though he be ignorant – is preferable to a child that is rude, unwashed, ill-natured, and yet becoming deeply versed in all the sciences and arts.[5]

Discipline and order in all affairs are of the utmost importance for the proper growth of the mental faculties of children. In families, everything should be done in a well-disciplined and orderly manner. Every action of the many daily actions, and every activity of the children's activities should be carried out properly. The basic causes of unruly behaviour should be cleverly uprooted by the capable hands of the knowledgeable mothers, so that the child, from his earliest years, can get used to order and organization in the family environment, and as a grown-up will shun everything which runs contrary to social well-being.

If the child does not get used to discipline and order in the family, if the times for sleeping and waking, for recreation and play, for work and rest, remain confused, if his precious life passes without a definite and clear-cut plan, if nothing has a specific place (for instance, while rummaging under the bed for a book he drags out his dirty socks) and part of the child's valuable time is always devoted to searching out shoes, hat, pen, and ink, only to find each of these items lying in a corner in a terrible condition – if this is the case, then how is it possible for him to develop into a punctual and well-organized adult, obedient to the rules which prevail in society?

Human nature is susceptible to change, for human

beings are, in general, the product of training. Our habits, traits, knowledge, and even our hopes and inclinations, are mainly the result of our training. Therefore if the mothers and educators know how their children should be, and with what thoughts and beliefs they should appear in society, they can take steps to provide adequate education, and firmly establish suitable traits and habits. Mothers, if they so wish, can accustom their children to discipline and order from childhood, and can put this educational point into practice with the utmost success. To attain this goal, however, it is essential to pay attention to certain matters.

1. The sleeping and waking hours of children, their recreation and play, their reading and writing exercises, their meal-times – in short, all their activities – should be geared to a definite programme from which there should be no deviation. Suppose a child is required to get up at six o'clock in the morning. He must be woken every day at that same hour; if at first he resists and wants to stay in bed, the mother should lift him up tenderly and compassionately, all the while patting him and showing him affection. In the beginning the child may resist strongly, but sooner or later this habit will become so established that he will get out of bed at the proper time without his mother's intervention. This occurs because traits and habits do not become second nature in human beings except through repetition.

On the same subject, it is important that the mother keep an eye on the time in the evening, and put the children to bed at a set time, in order that both their sleeping and waking may be carried out in a systematic manner. Naturally, mothers are aware that they should not tell their children terrifying fictional stories before putting them to sleep, as this excites the nerves and emotions. If children go to sleep feeling sad or nervous, it can prove harmful to their health. Nor should the children themselves read exciting books just before sleeping, especially love stories and romances (the perusal of which is always harmful for children and teenagers), as it is at this time that particularly unpleasant results can occur. During sleep, when the body is in a state of rest, the nerves should also be relaxed, the thoughts free, and the person happy. In general, it is much better if children do not tire themselves by studying just before sleeping, as this practice causes too much blood to accumulate in the area of the brain.

2. A child's books, note-books, towels, brush, toothbrush, clothing – all his belongings – should be kept in a specific place which no one else shares and where no one else interferes. Also, the child should be made responsible for its tidiness. In this way, a sense of responsibility is emphasized, and he gets used to both discipline and order. To carry out this task is possible for families in all strata of society. Even in small and simple rooms a corner can be set aside specifically for the children where they can put two or three small and inexpensive boxes in order to safeguard their belongings.

3. The fathers and mothers themselves should be orderly and well-organized, and should not purposely side-step their own regulations. In this way, their actions will serve as good examples for their children

to imitate and follow. The housewife should have a specific place for everything, and should try to keep household things in order. For instance, items which belong in the kitchen should not be taken to a different room, and whatever is supposed to be kept in the closet should not be put on the table, the mantel, or the window sills.

Even with respect to home decorations the mother should not be careless, and should not hang nonsensical and ridiculous pictures or crude quotations on the walls, so that in this way too, children will be exposed to a well-disciplined order in their surroundings, and will develop healthy interests and good taste.

4. With the utmost calmness and forbearance, but also with determination and steadfastness, mothers should guide their children to become orderly and well-disciplined in the home. They should not overlook any unruly behaviour or disorder whatsoever, but should, with soft words and a kind tongue, remind children of proper manners when it seems necessary to do so, as in the following example: A child arrives home from school, tosses his school bag in one corner, his hat in another, and in general totally ignores tidiness and order. The mother should immediately remind the child that such behaviour is displeasing, and that it is not correct for a polite and well-disciplined child to do such things. Then the mother should ask the child to pick up his bag and hat and put them in their proper places. The success of this depends upon the patience and forbearance of the mother. She should not give up easily, nor get upset at the first hint of indiscretion on the part of the child, but should stick to the virtues of kindness and mercy, and

resist resorting to anger and harsh language. Using patience, restraint, and steadfastness, mothers ought constantly to encourage their children to behave in a well-disciplined fashion at home. Experience has repeatedly shown that if parents put these suggestions into practice, their children will eventually become so accustomed to discipline and good organization that they will shun disorder until the end of their lives.

Many exponents of educational concepts try to attract parents closer to one of the ideals of training, which is 'beauty.' They hope – and expend much effort to this end – to implant in children from the earliest years a yearning to enjoy the beauty of the world of creation, to turn them away from that ugliness of chaos which is contrary to divine creation, and to nourish the children's souls in full accordance with their natural capabilities.

It is, of course, not possible in this brief reference to the subject of 'ideals' to delve into the examples and opinions of the philosophers of antiquity such as Plato and Aristotle, nor can we discuss the thoughts and views of Kant and his associates, nor those of learned and renowned contemporaries whose names are associated with the science of training and education. But it is clear that if the parents, and especially the mothers, accustom their children to order and organization in the home from childhood; if they never refrain from guiding them to observe a rational discipline in all matters; if they fix their sights upon all aspects of real harmony and true concord; and if they themselves do not deviate a hair's-breadth from order and sound discipline, then their children will more rapidly approach the ideal of beauty in their lives.

The Importance of Work for Children

Bring them up to work and strive, and accustom them to hardship.[6]

. . . all effort and exertion put forth by man from the fullness of his heart is worship, if it is prompted by the highest motives and the will to do service to humanity.[7]

We are all aware that work occupies a high position in the estimation of the learned throughout the world. When a person attains maturity and assumes his social responsibilities, he must become a source of social good, a useful element of society. His time may not be spent in idleness and complacency, even though he may be well-off, nor should the precious days of his life come and go in vain. Rather, he should become the cause of tangible benefits for his fellow men.

The foundation of this important undertaking must be established in the inner beings of children from early childhood so that they may be thoroughly prepared for work and purposeful activities. If the physical and mental faculties of children are not exercised and remain unequipped for work, there can be no doubt that, as adults, they will find themselves incapable of carrying out any job.

Families and schools sometimes try to work hand in hand to facilitate this difficult task for children, but unfortunately insufficient attention is often given to this important subject. For this reason we will give several suggestions here.

1. Mothers should not hesitate to entrust their children with work suitable to their capacity and ability. Idleness and self-indulgence must not be regarded with kindness, affection or sympathy, because anything,

even affection, when carried to excess, almost always proves to be harmful.

For example: young children, even from the ages of four and five, should develop the habit of doing daily chores by themselves (provided, of course, that assistance is not needed). When they get up in the morning, they can make their own beds; they can put on their own shoes and clothes, wash their hands and faces without the help of others, and pour tea for themselves. At lunch time, they can set and even wash their own dishes, and do related jobs. All these tasks should be carried out under the thorough care and guidance of the mother or the educator.

In large kindergartens in some countries, the author has seen with his own eyes how young children – even three and four-year-olds – with trembling hands but with evident joy and delight, do their own work under the ever-present supervision of the teachers. Obviously, the children should not be made weary; nor should work ever be allowed to be a burden to them. Instead, the work should be given to the children with great moderation, and in a disciplined and orderly fashion, as though it were an integral part of their lessons and exercises. Work in itself plays the part of an educator, inasmuch as the child's physical and mental faculties, while he is working, are busied with activities which will assist with his training.

In progressive kindergartens throughout the world, work is unanimously regarded as the best method for both the physical and the mental growth of children. Parents and educators, however, must take into account the varying capacities which children exhibit at different stages of growth.

2. Parents should know that children who are used to hardship, to extremes of heat and cold, and who are not pampered and over-protected, will be more vigorous and much more resistant to a variety of diseases. Children are on their way towards idleness and indolence if, by the age of six and seven, they are still not permitted to 'get their hands dirty,' as is so frequently the case; if, when they are eating and become thirsty, someone else gets up and hands them the water; if, when they feel inclined to do some particular chore, they are prevented. One mother may say, 'No, don't touch the cups. You might break them.' Another one says, 'Don't do that – you'll ruin your pretty dress.' Or a father may say, 'I've had to work hard all my life, and now that we've got a little money in the bank, I don't want to catch sight of you doing this kind of work.'

This brand of 'sympathy' and 'affection', which invariably leads to adversity and suffering for the unfortunate children, should be done away with altogether. It is not shameful to do physical work, and it is important that children get used to it from childhood.

3. By swimming, doing gymnastics, and taking long walks, children become stronger and more vigorous, and are better able to face the difficulties of life. Girls, of course, are not exempt from this, for the heavy burdens of life are shouldered to a greater degree by women than by men.

If children are disinclined to work at home when they are young, how then will they be able to withstand the arduous responsibilities they must eventually face? A young lady who has failed to acquire the habit of working, and has grown up luxury-loving and used to being pampered, will not be anything but a nuisance to her future family. Children, therefore, should accustom themselves to work and should never regard it as shameful. There can be no distinction between rich and poor in this matter; whatever the children are capable of doing for themselves should not be done for them by others.

Strengthening the Conscience

How excellent, how honourable is man if he arises to fulfil his responsibilities.[8]

It is . . . clear that the emergence of this natural sense of human dignity and honour is the result of education.[9]

The satisfaction felt as a result of completing an assigned task, and the regret experienced by failing to carry out a duty – these, in general, we regard as activities of the conscience. Most mothers and fathers are well aware that the conscience is the most important factor in determining whether or not moral principles are observed.

The writer urges that this statement be given careful attention, for the subject is of the greatest importance to society. If children are not trained to be dutiful from childhood, they will have acquired a moral short-coming which they will be unable to eradicate as grown-ups. And there can be no doubt that the most appropriate time for rectifying conduct is during the childhood years; when someone attains maturity, it will be exceedingly difficult to alter his behaviour and to correct any unsuitable characteristics.

When the affairs of a country run smoothly and that

country prospers, it is certain that its inhabitants are dutiful, and conscientiously attend to any social responsibilities committed to their charge. And in any country that is in a state of ruin and collapse, and the hopes and wishes of its inhabitants are utterly dashed, undoubtedly a significant number of its inhabitants are unruly, and their consciences are in a stupor.

This attitude of dutifulness should, therefore, be instilled in our children from the earliest years of their lives. It should be strengthened in an orderly manner. Some suggestions proposed by experts in the field of education follow.

1. The mother and father of a family should consult each other and carefully evaluate which duties are suitable for the children. Then, with the utmost kindness, they should bring up the matter with their loved ones. In a friendly but frank discussion, the necessity of everyone helping with the household chores should be explained; following this, each person's duties can be suggested. If any reservations are expressed by the children, the parents should listen carefully, and, if necessary, alter the earlier decision. After the matter has been settled and unanimously agreed to, then the parents should express their hopes that the tasks will be properly carried out.

2. Parents should never hesitate to remind the children that fulfilling one's duties ranks as one of the noblest of acts, that whoever is negligent in this matter will be ashamed and embarrassed in the sight of God and in the eyes of his fellow man, and that there are few things more blameworthy than procrastination and neglecting one's duties by making excuses.

3. To depict the consequences of failing to carry out one's duties, as well as the benefits of facing one's responsibilities, parents can make use of examples and stories based upon everyday occurrences.

4. The fact that a duty is performed well should be appreciated and the child encouraged.

5. Whoever neglects to do his share of the work should be counselled, and the situation corrected, but punishment must be meted out in such a gentle manner that the tender feelings of the child are not hurt, and no cause for jealousy arises.

6. During subsequent discussion periods, at which the father, mother and children are present, attention should be given to the performance of the duties which were assigned, so that any trouble spots, as well as what is expected of the children, are clearly understood. At that same meeting, the next programme should be drawn up, and new tasks assigned.

People who are unfamiliar with these suggestions may find this matter very odd, and perhaps laughable. But if careful attention is given, it will be seen that any matter with which the mind is unfamiliar seems odd at first, and its performance difficult or even impossible. But once the person gets used to performing the new task, it becomes perfectly normal and easy. For this reason, the writer requests that readers give serious consideration to this subject, and not dismiss it as unimportant.

Here is an example to help clarify the matter.

Imagine a family consisting of father, mother, and

three children, whose ages are six, nine, and eleven. In their home, there are many chores which the children are capable of carrying out, and which should be assigned to them. Naturally, those tasks can easily be taken care of by the parents or helpers, but from an educational point of view, it is essential that they be attempted by the children so they can gain practice in the affairs of life, become self-reliant, and not depend on others to do their work for them.

I recall reading about an extremely wealthy man who prevented his children from going to school. His reasoning went this way: 'Only those who aren't well-off should sweat and study to acquire knowledge. Why should my son learn geography, for instance, since he can travel wherever he wants, and others serve his every need?' Applying this same logic, some parents might say that their children should not have to work, if their family has a large amount of money.

Work trains a person, and gives him necessary practice. Work in itself is noble, and, when done in the spirit of service, is worship. 'No pain, no gain' is a popular saying. Assigning tasks to children has an educational aspect which should be used to advantage.

One evening, the parents set up a family discussion. The father says: 'There are five of us in our family, and there is always work to be done in and around the home. Let's talk for a moment about the type of work we have in our house, and who is able to do what.' At this time, of course, the importance of work and the necessity of everyone helping with it should be discussed, and it should be emphasized that these chores cannot be passed on to someone else.

'For instance,' one of the parents continues, 'in the morning, everyone should make his own bed. Everyone should replace his own towel, toothbrush, and hair brush and anything else needed for personal cleanliness. Everyone should clean and polish his own shoes, and then put away the shoe polish. No dust should be allowed to gather on the dressing tables, and the mirrors should always shine.

'At breakfast time, each of us can wash, dry, and put away his own plate and glass. At lunch time, the children should take turns setting the table and cleaning up the dishes afterwards. The one who tidies up should also put away the salt and pepper shakers, table napkins, and any clean dishes. And the same system also applies for the evening meal.

'Now that everyone knows what his duties are, everything can be done in an orderly fashion; your mother and father leave the performance of these tasks up to your consciences. As you love us and respect yourselves, you will do your chores as well as you can, for it is a very bad thing if a person says that he will do a certain task, but then leaves it undone. Can such a person be respected? Whoever performs his duty well sees that his mind is relaxed, that he has not given his work to somebody else to do, and that he has not deceived his mother and father.

'Whoever carries out his responsibilities has a tranquil conscience, and feels happy inside, whereas failure to do one's assignments torments the conscience. Dear children, I have read a story about the importance of doing one's duty, and now I want to tell it to you.

'You all know that at railway crossings and sidings there is always a guard whose duty is to signal the engineer to stop the train whenever there is danger. To do this, he waves a red flag. This guard is called the signalman, and if he is negligent, and fails to give a signal on time, the lives of all the passengers on the train will be endangered. This humble worker, as you can see, has a very heavy responsibility, and the least bit of neglect on his part could cost hundreds of lives.

'On one particularly cold winter day, a certain signalman was standing at his post. He was cold, and had no wood for the stove in his hut. A glance at his pocket watch told him that there was still half an hour before he had to flag down a train, and he thought to himself, "I have enough time to go and gather some wood; after all, it's not too far from here." He rolled up the red flag and put it in a special pouch attached to his belt; then he went towards the forest. But he became so involved in gathering wood that, by the time he realized he should be back at the siding, the whistle of the approaching train reached his ears. He looked at his watch, and saw that it was only a matter of minutes before the train was due at the crossing. The thought of the danger to the passengers made him feel dizzy and faint, but he managed to control himself, and started running towards the railway tracks with all his might. He reached the crossing as the train came closer and closer, but when he wanted to take out the red flag, the pouch was empty! The flag had fallen out while he was running! He sighed bitterly, and immediately reached in his pocket for a handkerchief. Taking a sharp knife which he always carried with him, he cut his hand, dyed the handkerchief red with his own blood, and frantically signalled. The engineer of the train spotted the red rag, and, realizing it was dangerous to go on, quickly brought the train to a stop. The signalman had collapsed by this time, and blood was flowing from his wound. A doctor on the train and several others rushed to his side and managed to stop the bleeding; after a short time, the man regained consciousness.

'And so, even though this man had been neglectful, nevertheless, due to his strong sense of duty, he managed to save the lives of many passengers, and avert an accident. It is said that the government of the day had a statue of this man made, and it was erected at the railway station in remembrance of his heroic act, and as an encouragement to others.'

Explaining Moral Subjects

. . . rear them so that from their earliest days, within their inmost heart, their very nature, a way of life will be firmly established that will conform to the divine Teachings in all things.[10]

Educationalists are of the opinion that verbal counselling, including explanations of spiritual matters and statements of moral truths, will not have the desired effect of refining children's conduct and rectifying their behaviour unless they are combined with other educational principles. In spite of this, we cannot altogether disregard the importance of this kind of training. Mothers and fathers should make the most of this method, and arrange orderly and regular meetings. The parents should sit with their children and carry on the discussion at a friendly level. The meetings themselves must be carefully planned, and each time, a different topic should serve as the basis for discussion. Whatever is necessary for the refinement of the children's character can be best explained through fables, examples, animal stories, parables, and narratives – all geared to the capacity, understanding, and perception of the children. Early in the evening is usually the best opportunity for these discussions since the children are free from their daily affairs, and everyone is normally at home at this time.

Nor can this point be overlooked: all parents, regardless of their level of education, are able to perform this task, for no special knowledge is required. With the utmost love and affection, the parents can gather their children together and teach them the essential moral points, clothed in the form of parables, and can counsel them, discouraging them from blameworthy things and encouraging them to do good things, all the while drawing their attention to the importance of praiseworthy behaviour in society.

Experience has proven this method to be beneficial in fostering sound moral attitudes in children. If these discussions are held regularly, are based on scientific principles and are not disrupted, the children will become used to them, and will look forward to them, and these evenings will leave a lasting impression on their memories. The children will be increasingly attracted to the home environment, and their minds and souls will become susceptible to beneficial and noble impulses. For instance, one evening the parents may gather the children around and begin:

'Dear children, you all know that God has created

us and all the creatures in the world. He is kind to all, shelters all, and provides for all, and is with us at all times. Whatever we do or say, and even whatever we think – He is aware of it, for one of His names is the All-Knowing. Since God desires good for us, and directs us only towards the right path, we must do our part, and sincerely try to obey His laws, and do whatever He has ordered us to do, and not do whatever He has forbidden, for our happiness and honour in this world, and in the world to come, depend only on this and on nothing else.

'The Prophets have said that whatever a person does not like, he should not wish for others. Whatever he does not want for himself, he should not want for others. This is called 'sympathizing', and it means that we should put ourselves in the other person's place so we can understand that whatever displeases us is displeasing to him too.

'For instance, since we like other people to do nice things for us and make us happy, we should do nice things for others too, and not hurt their feelings. If your friend at school speaks harshly to you or tears your note-book and breaks your pen, it is certain that you won't be happy; therefore, you should not do such things to your friend. And if your friend, because of a lack of understanding, does something that bothers you, then you should do good to him in return and show him courtesy and friendship. In this way, he will regret what he has done, will see how bad he has been, and will stop treating you and other people in that way.

'We should always be careful not to encroach on the life, the substance or the honour of anyone. We should cherish other people's lives and dignity as we do our own, so that we may become worthy members of mankind. These characteristics are called human perfections and moral virtues. Whoever does not possess these traits remains far from fulfilling his potential as a human being, and can even become worse than an animal, for animals never commit deeds as bad as those by untrained people.

'One of the human perfections which the founders of all religions have enjoined on us is that of reverence for parents, and it includes love, obedience, kindness, and consideration. Fathers and mothers have brought their children into being, and they face many hardships and sacrifice their comforts to ensure the happiness of their offspring. Children are indebted to their parents, and should be as obedient as possible to them. In childhood, in adolescence, and in adulthood they should revere their parents, have consideration for them, and not do anything which might break their hearts.

'In short, dear children, the only way to achieve true happiness and progress in this world and in the next is to avoid wrongdoing. This means that whatever God has forbidden, we should not do, and whatever He has commanded us to do, we should. Turning our backs on God's laws is the greatest cause of misfortune and unhappiness. When we get together again, we will speak more about this subject.'

Our invitation to parents to make use of this simple and straightforward method is coupled with a request that they do not disparage its use or dismiss it as impractical before first thinking it over and trying it out.

Teaching Children Manners

Courtesy is, in truth, a raiment which fitteth all men, whether young or old.[11]

Man is by nature a sociable creature. He spends his life not without human contact, but rather with his kith and kin. Association and friendship with others should begin during the childhood years.

In every nation there are certain customs which everyone in that country tries to observe; if anyone deviates too far from the norm and fails to behave towards his countrymen according to the mode of behaviour current amongst them, he will, of course, offend them, and as a result, friendly and harmonious relationships between him and others will not develop.

I have personally witnessed the extraordinary perseverence of parents in some parts of the world in teaching manners to their young children. The reason behind their effort is that any neglect in teaching social manners to children will lead to the belittlement of the parents in the sight of others – others who will see them as discourteous and devoid of good manners. It is to be regretted, however, that in some other parts of the world, parents give no importance to this matter; even if they themselves observe certain rules of social behaviour amongst themselves, they do not bother to teach them to their children. As a result, the children are not capable of associating with others properly, and at every step create a thousand kinds of embarassment for their parents.

Children who are taught polite forms of behaviour from the age of two or three (according to their capacity) are aware of the courteous manners which are required for greeting, for eating, for conversing, and so on; they are able to greet others in such a pleasant fashion as to be the cause of amazement.

Suppose you meet with a five-year-old child who has been taught proper manners. The moment she sees you, she greets you courteously. You ask her name, and she answers immediately; to your questions about her age, home, dolls, playmates, brothers and sisters, she replies as pleasantly as can be. At the table, her manners are the cause of wonderment; she never deviates from the acceptable mode of conduct, and is taught whatever is necessary for her age. She is so gentle with the guest that it seems as though bonds of friendship had existed between them for many years. In every sense of the word, the child is courteous, and possesses extremely good manners.

And now, if you meet a child who has not been so schooled, you will see the difference. The moment his eyes fall upon you he hides himself behind his mother and clings tightly to her dress. However hard the mother tries to bring him out of hiding, he stays put. After much fuss, he calms down, and you venture to ask his name. By way of an answer, he inserts his index and middle fingers into his mouth right up to the last joint, and fixes his gaze on the floor. If you are persistent and repeat your question a few times, he eventually presses on his mother's side with his free hand and whispers the instruction: 'You say it, you say it.' If it is a girl you are talking to, and you enquire whether or not she has a doll, she may very well reply, if she is the talkative type, 'I don't want to tell you. It's none of your business.' So many things of this nature occur that the mother feels obliged to punish the child, and God protect us if she starts crying.

A far more disturbing incident is to eat when an impolite child is at the table with you, for if the host, out of courtesy, places the choice piece of meat on your plate, the child, with his eyes, hands, shoulders and neck, makes so many motions indicating his preference for that very piece of meat that you are obliged to offer it to him.

These examples are not products of the imagination, nor are they exaggerated. On the contrary, they are quite true, and there are many others like them. It is clear, therefore, that teaching social manners and politeness to children from the earliest years is essential. A view commonly expressed by parents is that children should be trained only after they have grown up, but this thought is absolutely wrong. Admittedly, training children and rectifying their behaviour from childhood requires much trouble and effort, for if the task were easy, we would see no difference whatever between a cultured and an uncultured individual. If nature, experience, and the passage of time rectified man's conduct, then so much labour would not be needed; people would grow naturally like weeds. The animal aspect of man might, in fact, develop by itself, but very defectively. Evidences of intellectual capacity, however, are not possible except by means of continuous and orderly assistance from an educator.

Men are not less important than plants. If a tree is not trained by a gardener, if it is not taken care of, if it is deprived of water and fertilizers, and if weeds in its vicinity are not destroyed, then it will not produce delectable fruits. How, then, is it conceivable to leave a child to himself and allow him to waste the precious years of childhood and acquire nothing? After losing the 'capital' of his childhood in the 'gamble' of life, he will reach the age of maturity, and the most suitable period for his training will be well-nigh over; his mental capacity, in the opinion of physiologists, will atrophy.

Mothers and fathers would do well to consider once again these words which the poet Sa'dí wrote, almost seven hundred years ago:

Happiness will flee whosoever
is not trained in childhood.
Reflect: The green branch can be guided,
but the dry twig is straightened only by fire.

At this point, we put aside pen and paper, and bid farewell to our readers. If they find the thoughts contained in this book acceptable, and if they are able to make use of them, then this will be the writer's reward.

BIBLIOGRAPHY

Advent of Divine Justice, The. Shoghi Effendi. Wilmette, Illinois; Bahá'í Publishing Committee, 1939.

Bahá'í Education: A Compilation. The Research Department of The Universal House of Justice. Wilmette, Illinois; Bahá'í Publishing Trust, 1977.

Bahá'í World Faith. Selected Writings of Bahá'u'lláh and 'Abdu'l-Bahá. Wilmette, Illinois; Bahá'í Publishing Trust, 1943, 2nd edn. 1956, reprinted 1976.

Bahá'í Youth: A Compilation. National Spiritual Assembly of the Bahá'ís of the United States. Wilmette, Illinois; Bahá'í Publishing Trust, 1973.

Epistle to the Son of the Wolf. Bahá'u'lláh, translated by Shoghi Effendi. Wilmette, Illinois; Bahá'í Publishing Trust, 1941, 2nd edn. 1953, reprinted 1976.

Gleanings from the Writings of Bahá'u'lláh. Translated by Shoghi Effendi. Wilmette, Illinois; Bahá'í Publishing Trust, 1939, 3rd edn. 1976.

Hidden Words, The. Bahá'u'lláh, translated by Shoghi Effendi with the assistance of some English friends. London; Bahá'í Publishing Trust, 1932, reprinted 1975.

Paris Talks. Addresses given by 'Abdu'l-Bahá in Paris in 1911–12. First published 1912. London; Bahá'í Publishing Trust, 11th British edn. 1969, reprinted 1972.

Promulgation of Universal Peace, The. Discourses by Abdul Baha Abbas During His Visit to the United

States in 1912. Vol. 1, Chicago; Executive Board of Bahai Temple Unity, 1922. Vol. 2, Chicago; Bahai Publishing Committee, 1925. Published complete in one volume, Wilmette, Illinois; Bahá'í Publishing Committee, 1943.

Secret of Divine Civilization, The, 'Abdu'l-Bahá, translated by Marzieh Gail. Wilmette, Illinois: Bahá'í Publishing Trust, 1957, 2nd edn. 1970, reprinted 1975.

Selections from the Writings of 'Abdu'l-Bahá. Translated by a Committee at the Bahá'í World Centre and by Marzieh Gail. Haifa; Bahá'í World Centre, 1978.

Star of the West. vol. 9. Chicago; The Bahai News Service, 1918. Reprinted, in vol. 5. Oxford; George Ronald, 1978.

Tablets of Abdul-Baha Abbas. 3 volumes. First published 1909–16. New York: Bahá'í Publishing Committee, 1930.

Tablets of Bahá'u'lláh. Translated by Habib Taherzadeh with the assistance of a Committee at the Bahá'í World Centre. Haifa; Bahá'í World Centre, 1978.

REFERENCES

For full titles of the books referred to, please see the Bibliography. In the list of references, the page number is that of the last edition shown in the Bibliography.

1. SIX EDUCATIONAL COUNSELS

1. 'Abdu'l-Bahá, *Promulgation*, p. 163; *Bahá'í Education*, pp. 75–6
2. Bahá'u'lláh, Tablet of Wisdom, in *Tablets of Bahá'u'lláh*, p. 138
3. 'Abdu'l-Bahá, *Bahá'í Education*, p. 24
4. Bahá'u'lláh, *Gleanings*, CXXVIII, p. 277
5. 'Abdu'l-Bahá, *Selections*, p. 136; *Bahá'í Education*, p. 24
6. Bahá'u'lláh, Tablet of Tarázát, in *Tablets of Bahá'u'lláh*, p. 37
7. 'Abdu'l-Bahá, *Bahá'í World Faith*, p. 384
8. Letter on behalf of Shoghi Effendi to an individual believer, 9 July 1939, in *Bahá'í Education*, p. 66

2. RESPECT FOR CHILDREN

1. Bahá'u'lláh, *Hidden Words*, Arabic, no. 68
2. Bahá'u'lláh, Tablet of the World, in *Tablets of Bahá'u'lláh*, p. 88
3. 'Abdu'l-Bahá, *Promulgation*, pp. 175–6
4. 'Abdu'l-Bahá, *Selections*, p. 125; *Bahá'í Education*, p. 50
5. Letter on behalf of Shoghi Effendi to an individual believer, 26 January 1935, in *Bahá'í Education*, p. 63
6. 'Abdu'l-Bahá, *Promulgation*, p. 124
7. Bahá'u'lláh, Words of Paradise, in *Tablets of Bahá'u'lláh*, p. 69
8. 'Abdu'l-Bahá, *Tablets*, vol. 1, p. 45

3. METHODS OF DEALING WITH CHILDREN

1. 'Abdu'l-Bahá, *Selections*, p. 136
2. 'Abdu'l-Bahá, *Promulgation*, p. 433
3. 'Abdu'l-Bahá, *Bahá'í Education*, p. 24

4. 'Abdu'l-Bahá, *Selections*, p. 63
5. 'Abdu'l-Bahá, *Selections*, p. 135; *Bahá'í Education*, p. 43
6. 'Abdu'l-Bahá, *Selections*, p. 129; *Bahá'í Education*, p. 30
7. 'Abdu'l-Bahá, *Promulgation*, p. 50; *Bahá'í Education*, pp. 74–5
8. 'Abdu'l-Bahá, *Secret of Divine Civilization*, p. 96
9. 'Abdu'l-Bahá, *Tablets*, vol. 3, p. 663

4. SOME COMMON PROBLEMS

1. 'Abdu'l-Bahá, *Selections*, p. 130; *Bahá'í Education*, p. 31
2. 'Abdu'l-Bahá, *Bahá'í Education*, p. 23
3. 'Abdu'l-Bahá, *Selections*, p. 115
4. Letter on behalf of Shoghi Effendi to an individual believer, 9 July 1939, *Bahá'í Education*, p. 65
5. Bahá'u'lláh, *Gleanings*, CXXVIII, p. 278
6. 'Abdu'l-Bahá, *Promulgation*, p. 163; *Bahá'í Education*, p. 76
7. Bahá'u'lláh, *Gleanings*, CXXV, p. 265
8. Bahá'u'lláh, *Gleanings*, CLXIII, p. 342
9. 'Abdu'l-Bahá, *Secret of Divine Civilization*, pp. 97–8; *Bahá'í Education*, p. 17
10. 'Abdu'l-Bahá, *Selections*, p. 130; *Bahá'í Education*, p. 30

5. PRACTICAL CONSIDERATIONS FOR PARENTS

1. Bahá'u'lláh, *Gleanings*, LXXX, p. 154
2. 'Abdu'l-Bahá, *Bahá'í Education*, p. 48

6. CHILDREN AND FREEDOM

1. Bahá'u'lláh, *Gleanings*, CLIX, pp. 335–6
2. Shoghi Effendi, *Advent*, p. 28
3. Bahá'u'lláh, *Epistle*, p. 131
4. Bahá'u'lláh, *Hidden Words*, Persian, no. 56
5. 'Abdu'l-Bahá, in *Advent*, p. 27
6. Bahá'u'lláh, in *Advent*, p. 27
7. Shoghi Effendi, *Advent*, p. 25
8. 'Abdu'l-Bahá, *Selections*, p. 136

7. FOSTERING THE DEVELOPMENT OF CHILDREN

1. 'Abdu'l-Bahá, *Bahá'í Education*, p. 23
2. Letter on behalf of Shoghi Effendi to an individual believer, 16

November 1939, *Bahá'í Education*, p. 66

3. 'Abdu'l-Bahá, *Selections*, p. 139
4. 'Abdu'l-Bahá, *Selections*, p. 134
5. Letter on behalf of Shoghi Effendi to an individual believer, 13 November 1940, *Bahá'í Education*, p. 67
6. 'Abdu'l-Bahá, *Selections*, p. 126
7. 'Abdu'l-Bahá, *Tablets*, vol. 3, p. 606; *Bahá'í Education*, p. 50
8. 'Abdu'l-Bahá, *Selections*, p. 125; *Bahá'í Education*, pp. 49–50
9. 'Abdu'l-Bahá, *Bahá'í Education*, p. 51
10. Letter on behalf of Shoghi Effendi to an individual believer, 17 July 1938, *Bahá'í Education*, p. 63
11. Letter on behalf of Shoghi Effendi to youth attending Green Acre Summer School, 19 September 1946, *Bahá'í Youth*, pp. 7–8
12. 'Abdu'l-Bahá, *Promulgation*, p. 69

8. TRAINING CHILDREN IN THE SPIRIT OF RELIGION

1. Bahá'u'lláh, *Bahá'í Education*, p. 6
2. 'Abdu'l-Bahá, *Star*, vol. 9, no. 8, pp. 90–91; *Bahá'í Education*, p. 73
3. 'Abdu'l-Bahá, *Tablets*, vol. 3, pp. 578–9; *Bahá'í Education*, p. 25
4. 'Abdu'l-Bahá, *Secret of Divine Civilization*, p. 18; *Bahá'í Education*, p. 14
5. Bahá'u'lláh, Tablet of Ishráqát, *Tablets of Bahá'u'lláh*, p. 120
6. ibid. pp. 128–9
7. Bahá'u'lláh, *Gleanings*, CXXV, p. 265
8. Bahá'u'lláh, unpublished tablet quoted by permission of The Universal House of Justice
9. 'Abdu'l-Bahá, *Tablets*, vol. 2, pp. 262–3; *Bahá'í Education*, p. 50

9. A WELL-TRAINED MIND

1. 'Abdu'l-Bahá, *Selections*, p. 141
2. ibid. p. 144
3. ibid. p. 126
4. 'Abdu'l-Bahá, *Promulgation*, p. 47
5. 'Abdu'l-Bahá, *Selections*, p. 129
6. 'Abdu'l-Bahá, *Bahá'í Education*, p. 12

10. MORAL AND SOCIAL TRAINING

1. 'Abdu'l-Bahá, *Bahá'í Education*, p. 26
2. Letter on behalf of Shoghi Effendi to an individual believer, 11 January 1942, *Bahá'í Education*, p. 68
3. 'Abdu'l-Bahá, *Paris Talks*, p. 132
4. Letter on behalf of Shoghi Effendi to an individual believer, 9 July 1939, *Bahá'í Education*, p. 65
5. 'Abdu'l-Bahá, *Selections*, p. 135; *Bahá'í Education*, p. 43
6. 'Abdu'l-Bahá, *Selections*, p. 129; *Bahá'í Education*, p. 30
7. 'Abdu'l-Bahá, *Paris Talks*, pp. 176–7
8. 'Abdu'l-Bahá, *Secret of Divine Civilization*, p. 4
9. ibid. pp. 97–8; *Bahá'í Education*, p. 17
10. 'Abdu'l-Bahá, *Selections*, p. 126
11. Bahá'u'lláh, *Epistle*, p. 50